HOW TO HAVE WILLPOWER

ANCIENT WISDOM FOR MODERN READERS

■ ■ ■ ■ ■

For a full list of titles in the series, go to https://press
.princeton.edu/series/ancient-wisdom-for-modern-readers.

HOW TO HAVE WILLPOWER

■　■　■　■　■　■

An Ancient Guide to Not Giving In

Plutarch and Prudentius

Selected, translated, and introduced by
Michael Fontaine

PRINCETON UNIVERSITY PRESS

PRINCETON AND OXFORD

Published by Princeton University Press
41 William Street, Princeton, New Jersey 08540
99 Banbury Road, Oxford OX2 6JX

press.princeton.edu

GPSR Authorized Representative: Easy Access System
Europe - Mustamäe tee 50, 10621 Tallinn, Estonia,
gpsr.requests@easproject.com

All Rights Reserved

Library of Congress Cataloging-in-Publication Data

Names: Fontaine, Michael, editor, translator. | Plutarch. De vitioso
  pudore. | Plutarch. De vitioso pudore. English. | Prudentius,
  348- Psychomachia. | Prudentius, 348- Psychomachia. English.
Title: How to have willpower: an ancient guide to not giving
  in / Plutarch and Prudentius; selected, translated,
  and introduced by Michael Fontaine.
Description: Princeton, New Jersey: Princeton University Press, 2025.
  Series: Ancient wisdom for modern readers |
  Includes bibliographical references.
Identifiers: LCCN 2024040059 (print) | LCCN 2024040060 (ebook)
  | ISBN 9780691220345 (hardback) | ISBN 9780691220352 (ebook)
Subjects: LCSH: Virtue—Early works to 1800. | Temptation—
  Early works to 1800. | BISAC: PHILOSOPHY / History &
  Surveys / Ancient & Classical | SELF-HELP / Personal
  Growth / General | LCGFT: Essays. | Poetry.
Classification: LCC PA4374.M8 D75 2025 (print) |
  LCC PA4374.M8 (ebook) | DDC 179/.9—dc23/eng/20250129
LC record available at https://lccn.loc.gov/2024040059
LC ebook record available at https://lccn.loc.gov/2024040060

British Library Cataloging-in-Publication Data is available

Editorial: Rob Tempio and Chloe Coy
Production Editorial: Theresa Liu
Text and Jacket Design: Heather Hansen
Production: Erin Suydam
Publicity: William Pagdatoon and Carmen Jimenez

Jacket image: NiceProspects-Prime / Alamy Stock Photo

Printed in the United States of America

1 3 5 7 9 10 8 6 4 2

For—who else?—Faith

CONTENTS

ACKNOWLEDGMENTS

Frangar non flectar goes the mantra: I'll break but will not bend. Long after Latin had quit his land, this sentiment found its way to the Algerian poet Si Mohand (1848–1905). Recast as *a nerreẓ wal' a neknu*, it eventually became the battle cry of the Berber Spring. As an expression of sheer will, it can't be beat. But is it right for everyday life?

Flectar ne frangar reply others, no less wisely: I'll bend so I won't break. That's good too. But how much?

For balance and inspiration while exploring these thoughts, I would like to thank Peng Chen, Bob Weiss, and all the team at FLX Fitclub. Week after week we remind each other that life is a marathon, not a sprint, and keep each other smiling. For advice and encouragement on the texts, I once again thank Rob Tempio and Kim Hastings, the two referees, my mother Maryanne, and my friends Mark Saltveit and George Thomas (Quintus Curtius). Further back—fifteen years ago, somehow—Bert Adams-Kucik taught me what wise choices look like in adulthood. I remember her words every time I pass the statue of Hercules on Cornell's campus and the old story by Prodicus comes to mind.

In 2016, on the strength of some academic writings, I received the Thomas S. Szasz Award for Outstanding Contributions to the Cause of Civil Liberties. I knew Tom briefly before he ended his life, and he, more than anyone, would have appreciated the wit and clear-eyed wisdom that Plutarch and Prudentius bequeathed us here.

Ithaca, New York

INTRODUCTION

> *mens nostra quidvis videatur cogitatione posse depingere*
> The human mind seems able to create a mental picture of anything.
>
> —MARCUS TULLIUS CICERO,
> *On the Nature of the Gods* (1.15.39)

How do you feel when a smiling cashier flips an iPad screen toward you and offers you the option of adding a 25 or 30 percent tip to your bill?

And if you were given a piece of paper and asked to illustrate *willpower* and *addiction*, what would you draw?

This volume in the *Ancient Wisdom* series addresses both these scenarios. It brings together two meditations on resisting external pressure and internal appetites, and from different perspectives. The first is pagan, Greek, and by Plutarch, the greatest theorist of leadership and organizational behavior the ancient world knew. The other is Christian,

Latin, and by a late Spanish poet and civil administrator named Prudentius. Prudentius counsels active resistance to cope with temptation, whereas Plutarch counsels passive resistance in the face of injustice—indeed, as we shall see, he may have even invented the concept. And while Plutarch's advice comes in the form of a straightforward, self-help essay, Prudentius's is cast as a thrilling allegory of inner conflict modeled on Virgil's *Aeneid*. Titled *Psychomachia*—or in English, *Armageddon in Mind*—the poem pits avatars of willpower against our inner demons in an epic showdown between good and evil. The action is cinematic, the imagery ingenious, and the best part is that because abstract nouns are grammatically feminine in Latin, all the combatants are sword-swinging warrior women.

Both works are forgotten today. What unites them is a shared insistence on two points. First is that we *allow* pressure or temptations to get the best of us, indeed, in some ways even *want* it. And second, that we are not helpless victims of those pressures. We can *do* something about them.

INTRODUCTION

On Vice, Virtue, and Willpower

> When Hercules heard this, he asked, "Lady, what is your name?"
>
> "My friends call me Happiness," she replied, "but those who hate me have their own name for me: Vice."
>
> — PRODICUS, *On Hercules* (quoted in Xenophon, *Memorabilia* 2.1.26)

Vice—drinking, gambling, sex, smoking, shopping, porn—appears to be the self-destructive pursuit of happiness. Vices are the "demons" that we struggle with and sometimes succumb to. They're often criminalized. But what *is* vice, really? Is it sin, mental illness, or stupidity?

If I can't resist cupcakes and develop a weight problem, for example, what's to blame? Imps and gremlins, or brain impulses and ghrelin? Or is it simply that all things considered, I *prefer* overeating—for the taste, for the satiety, or because it helps me manage stress—to the inevitable consequences?

And conversely, if I want to regain control over my eating, how should I do it? Exorcise my demons ritually, or exercise habitually? Or should I try to excise those demons surgically, and undergo a bariatric or brain operation?

For these are, after all, the only three possibilities. We can demonize bad behavior as sin, blame it on Satan or witches, and seek theological relief. We can pathologize bad behavior as addiction, blame it on genes, chemicals and imbalances, or substances, and seek medical relief. Or we can take responsibility for bad behavior, blame it on no one but ourselves, and recognize, as psychologist Jeffrey Schaler maintains, that addiction is a choice. A stupid, stubborn, and difficult one, perhaps, but ultimately a choice.[1]

The collapse of the Western Roman Empire in the fifth century ushered in a new understanding of the world. That collapse, and the simultaneous rise of theological fanaticism in the Eastern Roman Empire, brought an end to the rationalist analysis of vice among the educated classes of Europe, North Africa, and the Middle East. As they abandoned classical philosophy, these regions reverted to universal belief in supernaturalism, mysticism, and mythology, and of a more pernicious kind than what had come before. Vice now became sin, a crime against God. It was invited or caused by Satan, his minions, and witches. As the Middle Ages went on, this supernatural worldview became entrenched and hardened. Toward the end, as the Middle Ages gave way in Europe to the Renaissance and Reformation, some 100,000 people were prosecuted for witchcraft. Between a half and a third of them—some

35,000 to 50,000 innocent human beings—were lynched or executed.[2] Less quantifiable but maybe more important is that countless individuals saw themselves as evil and in need of God's rescue.

This supernatural interpretation of vice dominated Europe for well over a thousand years. It fell away only in the seventeenth and eighteenth centuries, when a secular-medical view of vice as addiction and disease (mental illness) emerged and displaced it, dethroned the clergy, and gave rise to psychiatry. Dissenters can still occasionally be found, but in polite, public, and legal circles in western societies this medicalized worldview is every bit as entrenched and real today as its theological predecessor was four hundred years ago.[3]

What was the nature of vice before the rise and fall of Christianity? In classical Greece and Rome before the Middle Ages, it seems, all three interpretations of vice coexisted. As they always have and always will, the masses—and not only them—believed in malign spirits and witchcraft. (A 2021 YouGuv survey found that 43 percent of Americans believe in the existence of demons.[4])

Among the educated classes to which Prudentius belonged, the nature of vice was disputed along secular lines. Some doctors (and, exceptionally, the philosopher Plato) regarded vice as a mental illness. But most regarded it as a moral defect, a bad habit that one can successfully break through a reassessment of one's priorities and a concerted effort of the will.[5]

This was the view of all three major philosophical schools in Rome. For example, the first-century BCE Roman statesman and Academic-Skeptical philosopher Cicero declares,

> Stupidity (*stultitia*) unleashes and incites these perturbations to torment human life. They are like some kind of demons from hell (*quasi quasdam furias*), and we must resist them with all our might and every ounce of strength if we want to live this life we've been given in peace and quiet.[6]

Epicurean thought took a similar view. For Philodemus, Cicero's contemporary and the author of a multivolume treatise *On Vices and the Opposite Virtues*, vices amount to unrealistic expectations and a bad attitude. The proper "cure" is an attitude adjustment, which straight talk from a friend can help with.[7]

Writing a century later from the Stoic tradition, Seneca concurred. In a letter, he reports a distinction drawn by Posidonius, another contemporary of Cicero's and a leading apostle of Stoicism in the ancient world. Posidonius had noticed that in reference to a person, the word "drunk" (*ebrius*) is used in two different ways:

First, of a person who is loaded with wine and out of control, and second, of a person who gets habitually drunk and is at the mercy of the vice (*obnoxius ... vitio*).

"This is perhaps the earliest succinct distinction," write Peter Conrad and Joseph W. Schneider, "between one who has 'lost control' of behavior as a result of intoxication and one who has 'lost control' because of what came to be called 'alcohol addiction'." Accepting that distinction, Seneca declares that the latter behavior—getting drunk regularly—is "voluntary insanity" (*voluntaria insania*). For him it is a choice—a crazy choice, to be sure, but a choice all the same.[8] And, he believes, we can choose to stop it ourselves. (Which does not necessarily mean, of course, "all by ourselves.")

Such was the educated view of vice and its remedies before Christianity became allied with the state, ossified, and reinterpreted metaphorical "demons" as literal demons, and before the Enlightenment displaced the Christian view in turn and reinterpreted those "demons" as medical signs of chemical addiction or brain disease.

Aurelius Prudentius Clemens (348–after 405 CE), the Christian author of the poem on coping with addiction translated here, died on the threshold of the Middle Ages. It seems he wrote *Psychomachia* barely five years or fewer before the momentous sack of Rome in 410 CE, and he was the product of a classical Roman education. His poem thus captures a crucial moment in time. The new paradigm of vice was only beginning to displace the old, and for Prudentius, vice was still elective stupidity. It lies in our likes and dislikes, not in the substances we ingest or objects we consume, nor in our biological makeup. Prudentius would not have endorsed the saying "the Devil made me do it." He'd insisted on this point in an earlier poem titled *The Origin of Sin* (553–59):

> Why, though, ascribe every sin of the world and of men to an evil enemy's mischief? That's shifting the blame. In reality, sins grow up from our minds: they receive their birth, their substance, their power—all their identity, all of their strength—from the heart they're begotten of. He *is*, to be sure, the fuel and the cause of our sins, but [Satan] can only confuse or mislead us up to the point that we *want* it (*nos volumus*) . . .

We are *willing* sinners (*volumus*), says Prudentius, echoing Seneca's word "voluntary." And, as we shall see below, he is adamant that we can slay our demons and attain inner peace.

> "If you want to know how you really feel about someone, take note of the impression an unexpected letter from him makes on you when you first see it on the doormat [*today, he'd say 'inbox'*]."
>
> —ARTHUR SCHOPENHAUER

Have you ever asked yourself, *Why did I just do that?*

Letting yourself be bullied cuts to the heart of consent. The worst-case scenario is sex, but the issue comes up constantly in private and professional life. Social media has made clear that we *all* feel pushed around these days—from the top brass and the billionaires on down. And social media itself has made it easier than ever to pile pressure on someone. We can circulate petitions and open letters, form interest groups, mount campaigns, instigate moral panics, and issue demands for sweeping reform *right! now!* And all from the comfort of our couches.

We know this. So why do we still agree to or sign on to something when we *know* it's a mistake?

Plutarch has real insight into this difficult question. A Platonist like Cicero, Lucius Mestrius Plutarchus (c. 45–120 CE) is the first person in history to identify, name, and analyze the distinct feeling we experience when someone makes an improper request of us and we agree to it, *even though it's in our power to say no*. We comply not because we lack confidence, he says, but because we're too sensitive. We're people-pleasers. Pushovers. So we cave.

And for him, that's moral weakness.

Plutarch wrote three and a half centuries before Prudentius and he lived halfway across the Roman Empire, near Delphi in Greece. He was consumed with successes and failures of institutional leadership and sought to understand them. In the essay translated here, which probably dates to after 70 CE, Plutarch effectively says that by failing to say no, being bullied is our *revealed preference*. We would rather say yes to an unreasonable request than experience the shame, guilt, and potential embarrassment of saying no. The iPad tip request is paradigmatic of our current moment, but Plutarch identifies eight other scenarios that are every bit as familiar today as they were two millennia ago. Ask yourself: have you ever . . .

—voted for or supported a stupid policy?
—lent money to someone who will never repay it?
—written a letter of recommendation for someone unqualified?

—gotten someone an interview with an important, powerful, or famous person you know?
—hired someone unqualified for a job?
—lied for someone?
—rigged an award, a decision, or circled the
wagons against someone?
—said yes to sex you're not sure about?

If you did and you were not genuinely forced to—
that's different, of course—then Plutarch's essay is
for you.

When we surrender to such requests, an emotion that Plutarch calls "dysopia" is to blame. It
amounts to an oversensitivity to shame. We feel
ashamed to say no, so we say yes. And in order
to stop doing that, we need to recalibrate (so to
speak) our internal "shame-o-meter." In the best
spirit of ancient self-help writing, Plutarch offers
us a set of practical recommendations and steps we
can take to resist pressure and peer pressure, to
grow in confidence, and to stop saying yes against
our better judgment.

In the translation that follows, I leave the key
word, *dysopia*, untranslated. There are two reasons
for doing so. First, there is no equivalent word in
any language (previous translators have suggested
"compliancy" and "bashfulness," but it will soon
become clear why neither word quite gets it). By

adopting it intact, I would like to coin the word in English in exactly the sense Plutarch meant. From a practical point of view, it gives us a new term whose meaning we can agree on and which we can employ when we need to apportion blame for the consequences that follow it. Are consent and acquiescence the same thing, for example? Plutarch's word can help us tease that out and determine our next steps—for, as the saying goes, "If you wish to converse with me, define your terms."

The second reason is related and more important, and it is best illustrated by the Chinese doctrine of the Rectification of Names. As the story goes,

> A Chinese sage of the distant past was once asked by his disciples what he would do first if he were given power to set right the affairs of the country. He answered: "I would certainly see to it that language is used correctly." The disciples looked perplexed. "Surely," they said, "this is a trivial matter. Why should you deem it so important?" And the Master replied: "If language is not used correctly, then what is said is not what is meant; if what is said is not what is meant, then what ought to be done remains undone; if this remains undone, morals and art will be corrupted; if morals and art are corrupted, justice will go astray; if justice goes astray, the people will stand about in helpless confusion."[9]

If the misuse of language leads to corruption in morals, art, and justice, then reviving Plutarch's word for that awful feeling of pressure-but-not-coercion will help us begin rectifying social relations and dispelling the helpless confusion we have seen so much of in recent years.

> Καὶ σχεδὸν ἅπαντες, ὧν δὴ καὶ λόγος τίς ἐστιν
> ἐπὶ σοφίᾳ, ἢ μικρὸν ἢ μεῖζον, εἰς δύναμιν ἕκαστος
> ἐν τοῖς ἑαυτῶν συγγράμμασιν, ἀρετῆς ἔπαινον
> διεξῆλθον . . .
>
> Almost all who have written on wisdom
> have—either more or less, each to the best of
> their ability—extolled virtue in their writings.
>
> —SAINT BASIL OF CAESAREA (330–379),
> *How Young People Can Benefit from [Pagan]
> Greek Literature* (4.7)

Unlike Plutarch's easy-read essay, Prudentius's advice on vice is encoded in a miniature epic poem he calls *Psychomachia*. What does that title mean? In Greek, *psyche* denotes the mind and *mache* a struggle or fight, so a *psychomachia* is the effort to cope with mental problems—addiction, anxiety, explosive anger, and so on—and overcome them. Prudentius interpreted the word to mean a battle *of* your mind, *in* your mind, *for* your mind—or indeed, for your very life (which is another meaning of *psyche* in Greek). With its play on the literal and idiomatic senses of the expression "in mind," my own rendering *Armageddon in Mind* attempts to replicate these ambiguities.

And as noted earlier, the personified demons and coping mechanisms that do battle are all women. Prudentius calls them Virtues and Vices. Each side leads an army of soldiers, but for the most part we follow individual champions pitted against each other in single combats. The episodic nature of their bouts will bring to mind a video game such as *Mortal Kombat*, wherein we defeat one opponent only to immediately face another, deadlier foe at the next level. In particular, the Virtues square off against the Vices in the following seven bouts:

1) Faith vs. Worship of the Old Gods
2) Chastity vs. Lust
3) Patience vs. Anger
4) Humble Attitude vs. Pride
5) Temperance vs. Indulgence
6) Reason (and Action) vs. Greed (and Deceit)
7) Unity vs. Disunity

As we have seen, the Vices represent addictions, our worst instincts, while the Virtues correspond to what Abraham Lincoln called "the better angels of our nature." Like the T-cells in our immune system, they are internal defenses we can activate to stave off attack—except unlike T-cells, they're under our conscious control.

Three key words in the poem pose a challenge for the translator and should be noted here.

1) First is the word "virtue." In Latin, *virtus* originally meant "prowess" or "valor" or "heroism," originally in battle, and eventually in moral contexts. It was an active idea, even as a mental response to pressure, which is why Prudentius uses it above all to mean "willpower." In Christian times, the word was gradually reinterpreted in the same passive sense of "good (that is, restrained or obedient) behavior" that survives in English today. As will become clear, Prudentius plays on the conflict between the older and newer meanings of the word at several points.

2) Second, Prudentius announces that the struggle takes place "in the cave of the breast," by which he means the dark recesses of our heart or mind or soul or self or psyche. With some plausibility—think of how you feel when the plane hits turbulence—ancient thought located the

emotions in the breast rather than the brain. Although this different perspective poses a constant problem for translation, it also allows Prudentius to develop some magnificent imagery. For example, when Faith in the first battle omits to put on armor and trusts instead in her *validum pectus* (strong breast), Prudentius means both her pecs or chest, physically, and her "heart" spiritually.

3) Finally, in Latin and Greek the words for "spirit" and "breath" are identical (this is why "spiritual," "respiration," "perspiration," and "inspiration" share an obvious similarity). Hence, Prudentius repeatedly implies that a combatant's heavy breathing is a sign that she is "expiring"—that is, this is her "last gasp."

Christian and Jewish readers will detect many allusions to the Bible in *Psychomachia*. Some are pointed out in the notes, and readers will find many more listed in Pelttari's commentary. That said, you don't have to be a Christian or even believe in God to appreciate the poem. In fact, it may be even better if you don't, because other, equally valid meanings will suggest themselves to you.

A good example appears in the first battle, which pits Faith against Worship of the Old Gods. That latter name does not simply mean "paganism," though of course it does mean that. It also means "my old habits" or "my old enablers." And "Faith" does not mean merely Christian faith, though she obviously represents that, too, because faith has a special meaning in modern addiction treatment programs. For example, note what Conrad and Schneider write about Alcoholics Anonymous (1992, 90, emphasis original):

> The third AA step to recovery requires one to have "made a decision to turn our will and our lives over to the care of God *as we understood Him.*" The question of just how religious AA should be has always been somewhat controversial among its members. In an attempt to broaden its appeal to include virtually all spiritual experience, leaders were quick to point out that although the language of these steps sounds traditionally religious, such terms as "God" are to be interpreted loosely and on the basis of the individual's own spiritual biography. Attesting to the scope of this interpretation, [a former] chairman of the board of AA, says: "This turning over of self direction is akin perhaps to the acceptance of a regimen prescribed by a physician for a disease. The decision is made to accept reality, to stop trying to run things, and to let the 'Power greater than ourselves' take over."

"Faith" has this meaning for Prudentius, too. For him, as for Alcoholics Anonymous, it is the bedrock value and virtue that underpins all the rest. If we want to save ourselves from our worst instincts, we must first and foremost *believe* that we can do it (which, as the brilliant opening allegory about Abraham and Lot makes clear, does not mean recovery must be a solo effort). Willpower and effort are downstream of faith. Prudentius thus offers readers an empowering vision of what it means to struggle with self-destructive habits, both for Christians who struggle to decide how much responsibility they bear for their sins, and for all who struggle to believe that they are in control of their own destiny.

> "There is only one political sin: independence; and only one political virtue: obedience."
> —THOMAS SZASZ,
> *Ceremonial Chemistry* (2003, 175)

Legacy

The legacy of both works is profound, but in strikingly different ways. *Psychomachia* was widely read in the Middle Ages and proved enormously fertile for art history. Vivid illustrations of the battle scenes, apparently going back to an edition commissioned by Prudentius himself, are found in as many as twenty different manuscripts of the *Psychomachia*. With all its graphic violence, therefore, *Psychomachia* bids fair to be considered the world's first bestselling graphic novel.[10] And beyond the book illustrations, the battle of Virtues and Vices would inspire sculptural motifs on medieval cathedrals in western Europe. (The most dramatic examples can be seen on the west façade of the Strasbourg Cathedral, from which this book's cover illustration is taken, but many others exist.)

By contrast, although it was being recopied and perhaps even read in Byzantium, Plutarch's essay made no discernible impact on history until it was rediscovered and translated into Latin nearly fifteen hundred years later by the Renaissance humanist Desiderius Erasmus (1466–1536). In his introduction, Erasmus added a moving personal note about the merits of the essay (1526, 3):

> I translated this essay of Plutarch's all the more eagerly because in reflecting on the course of my life, I find that dysopia is responsible for more of the mistakes I've made than anything else. Nothing has turned out worse for me than all the concessions I've made, against my better judgment, to the importuning of friends.

Fifty years after Erasmus's translation appeared, in or around 1577, a fascinating samizdat essay came out in French. It was called *On Voluntary Servitude*, and it argued that the way to defeat tyranny—the nature of which had been an intense interest of Plutarch's—is to simply stop complying with injustice. Just stop. Do that, and the whole power structure will come crumbling down—no weapons nor bloodshed needed.

The author of this treatise had been an obscure young law student in sixteenth-century France named Étienne La Boétie (1530–1563, pronounced *la Bów-ay-zée*). He had died young, and, like Plutarch's, his essay made no discernible impact in his own time. A few centuries later, however, it was rediscovered and attracted the interest of Emerson, Thoreau, and Tolstoy. Not long after, via Tolstoy, Mahatma Gandhi and Martin Luther King Jr.—the world princes of nonviolent resistance—became acquainted with the ideas in the treatise. Hence, as Murray Rothbard correctly states in his introduction to La Boétie's essay, "La Boétie was the first theorist of the strategy of mass, non-violent civil disobedience of State edicts and exactions."[11]

This is the backdrop for a tantalizing remark that the French Renaissance essayist Michel de Montaigne (1533–1592) makes in chapter 10 of his essay *On the Education of Children*:

[Plutarch] says that the inhabitants of the Middle East came to be enslaved to one man because they could not pronounce one syllable: *No*. This saying of his perhaps gave matter and occasion to La Boétie to write his "On Voluntary Servitude."

Montaigne is referring to the joke in section 10 of Plutarch's essay translated here. Now, recent scholarship has shown that as a bare statement of fact, Montaigne's remark is unlikely to be true, and that the origins of La Boétie's essay are to be found in a Renaissance satire.[12] Nevertheless, to the extent that Montaigne's authority *made* his remark real, and that he was believed by all the great lights that followed him, one can argue that the principle of nonviolent resistance is to be found already right here in Plutarch. At any event, the germ of the idea is here for all to see.

These world-historical developments are all well and good, of course, but if your own goal is individual progress and personal development, then these two texts will make a more visceral and immediate impact. Arthur Schopenhauer once remarked that people can *do* what they will but cannot *will* what they will. He was right. We can't choose or opt out of our desires. We aren't all the same inside, either, which means that some things I find easy may be hard for you. But we do have choices. And "if freedom is the ability to make uncoerced choices," as Thomas Szasz noted,

> then man is born in chains, the innocent and helpless victim of internal passions and external controls that shape and possess him. Personal development, then, is a process of individual liberation, in which self-control and self-direction supplant internal anarchy and external restraint.[13]

This was the view of Plutarch and Prudentius all those years ago. Children and prisoners need not resist temptation because external controls do it for them. The rest of us have no such excuses. Plutarch, who believed firmly in progress and personal development, offers us a series of practical steps to grow a backbone and learn to stand up for ourselves. They're every bit as good today as they were nineteen hundred years ago. And Prudentius offers us an unforgettable tableau of the internal passions and anarchy we must learn to tame and supplant if we want to liberate ourselves and gain greater control and direction over our lives.

As we in our scientifically enlightened age read daily about a crisis of mental health sweeping society, particularly among the young, and as solutions are propounded and proffered with dubious backing, perhaps these ancient texts have something to tell us yet.

HOW TO HAVE WILLPOWER

Περὶ Δυσωπίας

Πλουτάρχου

[1] Ἔνια τῶν ἐκ τῆς γῆς φυομένων αὐτὰ μέν ἐστιν ἄγρια καὶ ἄκαρπα καὶ βλαβερὰν τοῖς ἡμέροις σπέρμασι καὶ φυτοῖς τὴν αὔξησιν ἔχοντα, σημεῖα δ' αὐτὰ ποιοῦνται χώρας οἱ γεωργοῦντες οὐ πονηρᾶς ἀλλὰ γενναίας καὶ πίονος· οὕτω δὴ καὶ πάθη ψυχῆς ἐστιν οὐ χρηστά, χρηστῆς δὲ φύσεως οἷον ἐξανθήματα καὶ λόγῳ παρασχεῖν ἐργάσιμον ἑαυτὴν ἐπιεικῶς δυναμένης. ἐν τούτοις τίθεμαι καὶ τὴν λεγομένην δυσωπίαν, σημεῖον μὲν οὐ φαῦλον, αἰτίαν δὲ μοχθηρίας οὖσαν.

τὰ γὰρ αὐτὰ τοῖς ἀναισχύντοις οἱ αἰσχυνόμενοι πολλάκις ἁμαρτάνουσι, πλὴν ὅτι τὸ λυπεῖσθαι καὶ ἀλγεῖν ἐφ' οἷς διαμαρτάνουσι τούτοις πρόσεστιν, οὐχ ὡς ἐκείνοις τὸ ἥδεσθαι. ἀναλγὴς μὲν γὰρ ὁ ἀναιδὴς πρὸς τὸ αἰσχρόν, εὐπαθὴς δὲ καὶ πρὸς τὸ φαινόμενον

RESISTING PRESSURE
Dysopia (On Caving)

PLUTARCH

You Are Too Sensitive

Dysopia Is an Excess of Shame

[1] Some things that grow from the earth are just wild and bear no fruit, and their spread harms cultivated plants and crops. Farmers take them as signs, though, that the soil is healthy and productive rather than poor.

Well, negative emotions are like that. They aren't good, but they're "outgrowths" of a good nature, a nature that can make itself relatively open to reason. Among them I put what's called "dysopia." It's not a bad sign, but it leads to terrible behavior.

You see, people with a healthy sense of shame often make the same mistakes that shameless people do, except they get upset and distressed at their lapses, while the latter enjoy theirs. That's because the shameless person is untroubled by a shameful action, whereas the pushover is highly sensitive to even the appearance of a shameful action.

αἰσχρὸν ὁ εὐδυσώπητος· ὑπερβολὴ γὰρ τοῦ αἰσχύνεσθαι τὸ δυσωπεῖσθαι. διὸ καὶ οὕτως κέκληται, τρόπον τινὰ τοῦ προσώπου τῇ ψυχῇ συνδιατρεπομένου
καὶ συνεξατονοῦντος. ὡς γὰρ τὴν κατήφειαν ὁρίζονται
λύπην κάτω βλέπειν ποιοῦσαν, οὕτω τὴν αἰσχυντηλίαν
μέχρι τοῦ μηδὲ ἀντιβλέπειν τοῖς δεομένοις ὑπείκουσαν
δυσωπίαν ὠνόμασαν.

   ὅθεν ὁ μὲν ῥήτωρ τὸν ἀναίσχυντον οὐκ ἔφη κόρας
ἐν τοῖς ὄμμασιν ἔχειν ἀλλὰ πόρνας· ὁ δ᾽ εὐδυσώπητος
αὖ πάλιν ἄγαν τὸ θῆλυ τῆς ψυχῆς καὶ τρυφερὸν ἐμφαί-
νει διὰ τῆς ὄψεως, τὴν ὑπὸ τῶν ἀναισχύντων ἧτταν
αἰσχύνην ὑποκοριζόμενος. ὁ μὲν οὖν Κάτων ἔλεγεν
τῶν νέων μᾶλλον ἀγαπᾶν τοὺς ἐρυθριῶντας ἢ τοὺς
ὠχριῶντας, ὀρθῶς ἐθίζων καὶ διδάσκων τὸν ψόγον
μᾶλλον ἢ τὸν πόνον δεδιέναι καὶ τὴν ὑποψίαν μᾶλλον
ἢ τὸν κίνδυνον· οὐ μὴν ἀλλὰ καὶ τοῦ πρὸς τὸν ψόγον
ὑπόπτου καὶ ψοφοδεοῦς τὸ ἄγαν ἀφαιρετέον, ὡς οὐχ
ἧττον ἔνιοι πολλάκις ἀκοῦσαι κακῶς ἢ παθεῖν δείσαντες
ἀπεδειλίασαν καὶ προήκαντο τὸ καλὸν οὐ δυνηθέντες
ὑπομεῖναι τὸ ἄδοξον.

[2] Οὔτε δὴ τούτους περιοπτέον οὕτως ἀσθενῶς ἔχο-
ντας οὔτ᾽ αὖ πάλιν ἐκείνην ἐπαινετέον τὴν ἄτρεπτον
καὶ ἀτενῆ διάθεσιν, ἀλλ᾽ ἐμμελῆ τινα μηχανητέον σύ-

I say all this because *dysopia is an undue sensitivity to shame*. In fact, that's why it's called dys"op"ia, since our face or countenance (*op*) somehow cringes and falls along with our feelings.

You see, just as feeling downcast is defined as unhappiness that causes us to look downward, so dysopia is the name for a sense of insecurity that's so powerful that it stops us from looking our petitioner in the eye. And that explains why one wit quipped that shameless people "have hussies, not pupils, in their eyes."[14] Whereas, again, the face of the pushover shows all too clearly the cowardice and effeminacy in his heart, though he euphemizes his capitulation to shameless requests as "being flexible."

I know Cato [the Elder] used to say he preferred young men who blushed to those who blanched, and he was right to teach us to fear criticism more than hard work, and suspicion more than danger. Still, we really must stop being overly worried about criticism and panicking. People too often wimp out because they're more afraid of mean words than physical harm, and, because they can't stomach getting called names, they sacrifice a noble cause.

[2] Well, we shouldn't condone such weakness from these people, but, by the same token, we also shouldn't endorse the other extreme of complete inflexibility. Instead, we ought to formulate a

γκρασιν ἀμφοῖν, τοῦ μὲν ἀτενοῦς ἄγαν τὴν ἀναίδειαν,
τοῦ δὲ ἐπιεικοῦς σφόδρα τὴν ἀσθένειαν ἀφαιροῦσαν.
ᾗ καὶ τὸ θεράπευμα δυσχερὲς καὶ οὐκ ἀκίνδυνος ἡ τῶν
τοιούτων πλεονασμῶν κόλουσις [Becchi: κόλασις
"chastisement" vulgate].

– ὡς γὰρ ὁ γεωργὸς ἄγριον μὲν ἐκκόπτων βλάστημα καὶ ἀγεννὲς αὐτόθεν ἀφειδῶς ἐμβαλὼν
τὸ σκαφεῖον ἀνέτρεψε τὴν ῥίζαν ἢ πῦρ προσα-
γαγὼν ἐπέκαυσεν, ἀμπέλῳ δὲ προσιὼν τομῆς
δεομένῃ καὶ μηλέας ἤ τινος ἐλαίας ἁπτόμενος
εὐλαβῶς ἐπιφέρει τὴν χεῖρα, δεδιὼς μή τι τοῦ
ὑγιαίνοντος ἀποτυφλώσῃ,
– οὕτως ὁ φιλόσοφος φθόνον μὲν ἐξαιρῶν νέου
ψυχῆς, ἀγεννὲς βλάστημα καὶ δυστιθάσευτον, ἢ
φιλαργυρίαν ἄωρον ἢ φιληδονίαν ἐπικόπτων
ἀκόλαστον αἱμάσσει καὶ πιέζει καὶ τομὴν ποιεῖ καὶ
οὐλὴν βαθεῖαν· ὅταν δὲ τρυφερῷ μέρει ψυχῆς καὶ
ἁπαλῷ κολούοντα προσαγάγῃ λόγον, οἷόν ἐστι
τὸ δυσωπούμενον καὶ διατρεπόμενον, εὐλαβεῖται
μὴ λάθῃ τούτοις συναποκόψας τὸ αἰδούμενον.

καὶ γὰρ αἱ τίτθαι τῶν βρεφῶν ἐκτρίβουσαι πολλάκις
τὸν ῥύπον ἑλκοῦσιν ἐνίοτε τὴν σάρκα καὶ βασανίζουσιν.
ὅθεν οὐ δεῖ τῶν νέων παντάπασιν ἐν χρῷ τὴν δυσωπίαν
ἐκτρίβοντας ὀλιγώρους ποιεῖν καὶ λίαν ἀτρέπτους·

well-balanced blend of both—a blend that removes the callous indifference of excessive rigidity *and* the weakness of extreme "flexibility."

So the cure is difficult, and the pruning of such excesses involves some risk, too. You see, when

– a gardener is clearing overgrown and unwanted weeds, he'll simply stick his shovel in the ground and rip the roots right up, or apply a flame and torch them. When he comes to resect a grapevine, though, or an apple or olive tree, he handles it carefully, in fear of cutting a bud out from the healthy part. In the same way, when

– a therapist is ridding a teenage soul of malice—a stubborn and unwanted growth—or clearing signs of hedonism or greed, he'll slash, bear down, resect the skin, and leave a deep scar. When he applies a pointed remark to a delicate and tender part of the soul, though— such as the part that causes feelings of awkwardness and turns us into pushovers—he's careful not to accidentally cut all sense of shame out along with it.

Likewise, when nannies scrub babies too often, they sometimes tear their skin and hurt them. This suggests that there's no need to scrub teenagers of dysopia down to the quick and leave them too rigid and unfeeling. No, we have to get rid of it in the

ἀλλ᾽ ὥσπερ οἱ καταλύοντες οἰκίας ἱεροῖς γειτνιώσας
τά γε συνεχῆ καὶ πλησίον ἐῶσι καὶ διερείδουσιν, οὕτω
δεῖ τὴν δυσωπίαν κινεῖν, δεδιότας συνεφελκύσασθαι
τὰ ὁμοροῦντα τῆς αἰδοῦς καὶ τῆς ἐπιεικείας καὶ τῆς
ἡμερότητος, οἷς ὑποδέδυκε καὶ προσπέπλεκται, κολα-
κεύουσα τὸν εὐδυσώπητον ὡς φιλάνθρωπον καὶ πο-
λιτικὸν καὶ κοινὸν ἔχοντα νοῦν καὶ οὐκ ἄτεγκτον οὐδὲ
αὐθέκαστον. ὅθεν εὐθὺς οἱ Στωϊκοὶ καὶ τῷ ῥήματι τὸ
αἰσχύνεσθαι καὶ δυσωπεῖσθαι τοῦ αἰδεῖσθαι διέστη-
σαν ἵνα μηδὲ τὴν ὁμωνυμίαν τῷ πάθει πρόφασιν τοῦ
βλάπτειν ἀπολίπωσιν.

ἀλλ᾽ ἡμῖν χρῆσθαι τοῖς ὀνόμασιν ἀσυκοφαντήτως
δότωσαν, μᾶλλον δὲ Ὁμηρικῶς· καὶ γὰρ ἐκεῖνος εἶπεν

αἰδώς, ἥ τ᾽ ἄνδρας μέγα σίνεται ἠδ᾽ ὀνίνησι.

καὶ οὐ κακῶς τὸ βλάπτον αὐτῆς πρότερον εἶπεν·
γίνεται γὰρ ὠφέλιμος ὑπὸ τοῦ λόγου τὸ πλεονάζον
ἀφελόντος καὶ τὸ μέτριον ἀπολιπόντος.

[3] Πρῶτον οὖν τοῦτο δεῖ πείθεσθαι τὸν ὑπὸ πολλῆς
δυσωπίας βιαζόμενον, ὅτι πάθει βλαβερῷ συνέχεται,

same way that builders do when they're demolishing a house which abuts a temple: they leave alone the parts that are touching or practically touching the temple, and reinforce them. We don't want to remove along with dysopia adjacent concepts which underlie and entwine it, such as a healthy sense of shame, and reasonableness, and niceness—concepts that flatter the pushover as "understanding" and "politic" and "empathetic" and not "stubborn" or "blunt." (That's why the Stoics distinguished the word *dysopia* from *shame* and *a healthy sense of shame*; their goal was to deprive the emotion of even the same name as a pretext for doing harm.)

Still, if they'll allow it, let's not get pedantic about nomenclature. Let's simply follow Homer, since he said [in fact Hesiod, *Works and Days* 318 ~ Homer, *Iliad* 24.44–45]:

> Shame, which does men both great harm and great
> help.

He wasn't wrong to mention the harm first, incidentally, since shame only becomes healthy once reason has removed the excess and leaves us with the right amount.

[3] Therefore, when someone is acting under the influence of dysopia, the first thing to do is make them understand that they're suffering from

καλὸν δὲ τῶν βλαβερῶν οὐδέν, οὐδὲ δεῖ τοῖς ἐπαίνοις
κηλούμενον ἥδεσθαι κομψὸν καὶ ἱλαρὸν ἀντὶ σεμνοῦ
καὶ μεγάλου καὶ δικαίου προσαγορευόμενον, μηδ᾽
ὥσπερ ὁ Εὐριπίδου Πήγασος

ἔπτησσ᾽ ὑπείκων μᾶλλον ἢ μᾶλλον θέλοι

τῷ Βελλεροφόντῃ, τοῖς δεομένοις ἑαυτὸν ἐκδιδόναι
καὶ συνεκταπεινοῦν φοβούμενον ἀκοῦσαι τὸ "σκλη-
ρός γε καὶ ἀπηνής."

τῷ μὲν γὰρ Αἰγυπτίῳ Βοκχόριδι φύσει χαλεπῷ
[vulgate: perhaps γαληνῷ "gentle" Pelttari per lit-
teras] γενομένῳ τὴν ἀσπίδα λέγουσιν ὑπὸ τῆς Ἴσιδος
ἐπιπεμφθεῖσαν καὶ τῇ κεφαλῇ περιελιχθεῖσαν ἄνω-
θεν ἐπισκιάζειν ἵνα κρίνῃ δικαίως· ἡ δέ τοι δυσωπία
τοῖς ἀτόνοις καὶ ἀνάνδροις ἐπικειμένη καὶ πρὸς μηδὲν
ἀνανεῦσαι μηδὲ ἀντειπεῖν ἰσχύουσα καὶ δικάζοντας
ἀποτρέπει τοῦ δικαίου καὶ συμβουλεύοντας ἐπιστο-
μίζει καὶ λέγειν πολλὰ καὶ πράττειν ἀναγκάζει τῶν
ἀβουλήτων· ὁ δὲ ἀγνωμονέστατος ἀεὶ τοῦ τοιούτου
δεσπότης ἐστὶ καὶ κρατεῖ τῷ μὴ αἰδεῖσθαι τὸ αἰδούμενον ἐκβιαζόμενος.

a pathological emotion, and that nothing pathological is good. They can't let themselves get seduced by praises; they shouldn't want to be called "nice" and "good" rather than "important" and "impressive" and "fair-minded." They shouldn't be like Pegasus in Euripides's play, who, for Bellerophon [fr. 309 Nauck]

> bowed and yielded at his rider's will.

They can't surrender to bullies and stoop to their level because they're afraid of getting called (predictably) "callous and cruel."

Because King Bakenranef of Egypt was a naturally harsh man, legend has it that Isis sent a cobra down to curl around his head and loom out over it and make sure the king judged disputes fairly.[15]

Dysopia terrorizes weaklings and wimps in a similar way. Because it lacks the strength to deny or refuse anything, it stops them from settling disputes fairly, from speaking up in meetings, and it forces them to say and do many things they disagree with. The most unreasonable person is always the master of such a man; his shamelessness tyrannizes the first man's sense of shame and overpowers it.

Consequences in Sexual Relations

Plutarch now comes to the delicate topic of consent in sexual relations. Because many Greek men were bisexual, he first addresses "pederasty"—that is, the

11

ὅθεν ὥσπερ χωρίον ὕπτιον καὶ μαλακὸν ἡ δυσωπία
μηδεμίαν ἔντευξιν ἐξῶσαι μηδὲ ἀποστρέψαι δυναμένη
τοῖς αἰσχίστοις βάσιμός ἐστι πάθεσι καὶ πράγμασι· κακὴ
μὲν γὰρ αὕτη παιδικῆς φρουρὸς ἡλικίας, ὡς ἔλεγε
Βροῦτος οὐ δοκεῖν αὐτῷ καλῶς τὴν ὥραν διατεθεῖ-
σθαι τὸν πρὸς μηδὲν ἀρνούμενον· κακὴ δὲ θαλάμου
καὶ γυναικωνίτιδος ἐπίτροπος, ὡς φησιν ἡ παρὰ τῷ
Σοφοκλεῖ μετανοοῦσα πρὸς τὸν μοιχόν

ἔπεισας ἐξέθωψας.

ὥσθ' ἡ δυσωπία προσφέρουσα [Becchi 1996: προσδι-
αφθείρασα "further corrupts" vulgate] τὸ ἀκόλαστον,
ἀνώχυρα πάντα καὶ ἄκλειστα καὶ κατάντη προδίδωσι
τοῖς ἐπιτιθεμένοις. καὶ διδόντες μὲν αἱροῦσι τὰς βδε-
λυρωτάτας, τῷ δὲ πείθειν καὶ δυσωπεῖν πολλάκις κατ-
εργάζονται καὶ τὰς ἐπιεικεῖς.

normalized sexual abuse of boys by grown men within stable romantic relationships. In such relationships men typically courted boys, offering them gifts or opportunities in exchange for their favors. Plutarch then addresses heterosexual relations, and here readers should be aware that in classical Greece, as in some Middle Eastern countries today, respectable women were routinely secluded within the house, allowed outdoors only with a male relative chaperone, and they typically veiled themselves when they did go out.[16]

And so, being unable to reject or refuse any request, dysopia, like flat and soft terrain, risks being walked all over and victimized in the most shameful ways. You see, dysopia is a poor protector of one's boyhood, which is why Brutus used to say he didn't think a man who denied nothing had managed that period well [*Life of Brutus* 6.9 (986E)].

It's also a poor guardian of the bedroom and harem, as the regretful woman in Sophocles's play says to her seducer [fr. 857 Radt],

You sweet-talked me, you *tricked* me . . . !

As a result, by inducing a compromise of principles, dysopia delivers everything up to its attackers — unsecured, unlocked, a downhill slide. And while gifts win over loose women, persuasion and pressure work all too often even on women of virtue.[17]

13

(ἐῶ δὲ τὰς εἰς τὰ χρήματα βλάβας ὑπὸ τοῦ δυσωπεῖσθαι, δανειζόντων οἷς ἀπιστοῦσιν, ἐγγυωμένων οὓς οὐ θέλουσιν, ἐπαινούντων μὲν τὸ "ἐγγύα πάρα δ᾽ ἄτα," χρῆσθαι δ᾽ αὐτῷ περὶ τὰ πράγματα μὴ δυναμένων.)

[4] Ὅσους δ᾽ ἀνήρηκε τοῦτο τὸ πάθος οὐκ ἄν τις ἐξαριθμήσαιτο ῥᾳδίως. καὶ γὰρ ὁ Κρέων πρὸς τὴν Μήδειαν εἰπών,

κρεῖσσον δέ μοι νῦν πρός σ᾽ ἀπεχθέσθαι, γύναι,
ἢ μαλθακισθένθ᾽ ὕστερον μέγα στένειν,

ἄλλοις ἐγνωμολόγησεν, αὐτὸς δὲ τῆς δυσωπίας ἥττων γενόμενος καὶ μίαν ἡμέραν αἰτουμένῃ δοὺς ἀπώλεσε τὸν οἶκον.

ἔνιοι δὲ καὶ σφαγὰς ὑφορώμενοι καὶ φαρμακείας διετράπησαν.

– οὕτω παραπώλετο Δίων, οὐκ ἀγνοήσας ἐπιβουλεύοντα Κάλλιππον ἀλλ᾽ αἰσχυνθεὶς φυλάττεσθαι φίλον ὄντα καὶ ξένον·
– οὕτως Ἀντίπατρος ὁ Κασάνδρου Δημήτριον καλέσας ἐπὶ δεῖπνον, εἶτα κληθεὶς τῇ ὑστεραίᾳ πρὸς αὐτὸν ᾐδέσθη πεπιστευμένος ἀπιστεῖν, καὶ πορευθεὶς ἐσφάγη μετὰ τὸ δεῖπνον.

(I'll pass over the monetary losses caused by caving to pressure—the lending money to people you don't trust, the cosigning loans you don't want to, and endorsing the saying "Give a guarantee, go broke," but being unable to heed it in practice.)

[4] It would be difficult to count all the lives this emotion has ruined. You see, when Creon told Medea [Euripides *Medea* 290–291]—

Better for me to have your hate right now,
woman, than to go soft and groan regret

—he gave sage advice to others but succumbed to pressure himself, and by granting her request for a day's reprieve he destroyed his world.

Even some who suspected assassination or a poisoning attempt have refused to face it. For example:

- Dion perished—not out of ignorance at Callippus's plot, but because he felt ashamed to take protective measures against a close friend.
- Antipater, the son of Cassander, invited Demetrius to dinner, and was invited in return the following day. He was ashamed not to trust a man who'd trusted him, so he went—and was murdered after the meal.

– Ἡρακλέα δὲ τὸν Ἀλεξάνδρῳ γενόμενον ἐκ
Βαρσίνης ὡμολόγησε μὲν Κασάνδρῳ Πολυ-
πέρχων ἀναιρήσειν ἐπὶ ταλάντοις ἑκατόν, εἶτα
ἐπὶ δεῖπνον ἐκάλει· τοῦ δὲ μειρακίου τὴν κλῆσιν
ὑφορωμένου καὶ δεδοικότος, ἄλλως δὲ προ-
φασιζομένου μαλακώτερον ἔχειν, ἐλθὼν ὁ Πο-
λυπέρχων, "πρῶτον," εἶπεν, "ὦ παῖ, μιμοῦ τοῦ
πατρὸς τὸ εὔκολον καὶ φιλέταιρον, εἰ μὴ νὴ Δία
δέδοικας ἡμᾶς ὡς ἐπιβουλεύοντας." αἰδεσθεὶς
ἠκολούθησεν ὁ νεανίσκος· οἱ δὲ δειπνίσαντες
αὐτὸν ἐστραγγάλισαν.

οὐ γελοῖον οὖν, ὥς φασι, οὐδὲ ἀβέλτερον, ἀλλὰ σοφὸν
τὸ τοῦ Ἡσιόδου·

τὸν φιλέοντ᾽ ἐπὶ δαῖτα καλεῖν, τὸν δ᾽ ἐχθρὸν ἐᾶσαι.

μὴ δυσωποῦ τὸν μισοῦντα μηδ᾽ ὑπαίκαλλε πιστεύειν
δοκοῦντα· κληθήσῃ γὰρ καλέσας καὶ δειπνήσεις ἂν
δειπνίσῃς, ὥσπερ βαφὴν τὴν φυλάττουσαν ἀπιστίαν
μαλαχθεῖσαν αἰσχύνῃ προέμενος.

– Polyperchon cut a deal with Cassander to get rid of Heracles of Macedon, Alexander's son by Barsine, for a million dollars, so he began inviting him to dinner.[18] But the young man was suspicious and afraid, and kept claiming he felt unwell. Polyperchon went to see him and said, "Now, my boy, you should emulate your father's agreeableness and sociability — unless, of course, you're worried that I'm plotting something!" The young man was shamed into going, and after serving him dinner, they strangled him.

It isn't funny or ridiculous (as some claim), therefore, but wise, when Hesiod says [*Works and Days* 342]:

Invite your friend to a feast, but give your enemy a pass.

Don't get pushed around by an adversary — but also, don't kowtow if he seems to trust you. See, when you invite *him* over, he'll invite *you*, and once he's dined with *you*, then you'll go dine with *him* — and all because you let your sense of shame blunt the protective edge of distrust.

[5] Ὡς οὖν πολλῶν κακῶν αἴτιον τὸ νόσημα τοῦτο ὂν
πειρατέον ἀποβιάζεσθαι τῇ ἀσκήσει, πρῶτον ἀρξαμέ-
νους, ὥσπερ οἱ τἆλλα μελετῶντες, ἀπὸ τῶν μικρῶν
καὶ μὴ σφόδρα δυσαντιβλέπτων. οἷον . . .

— ἐν δείπνῳ προπίνει τις ἄδην ἔχοντι· μὴ δυσωπηθῇς μηδὲ προσβιάσῃ σαυτόν, ἀλλὰ κατάθου
τὸ ποτήριον.
— αὖθις ἕτερος παρακαλεῖ κυβεύειν παρὰ πότον·
μὴ δυσωπηθῇς μηδὲ δείσῃς σκωπτόμενος· ἀλλ᾽
ὥσπερ Ξενοφάνης Λάσου τοῦ Ἑρμιονέως μὴ
βουλόμενον αὐτῷ συγκυβεύειν δειλὸν ἀποκα-
λοῦντος ὁμολόγει καὶ πάνυ δειλὸς εἶναι πρὸς τὰ
αἰσχρὰ καὶ ἄτολμος.
— πάλιν ἀδολέσχῃ συνήντηκας ἐπιλαμβανομένῳ
καὶ περιπλεκομένῳ· μὴ δυσωπηθῇς ἀλλὰ δια-
κόψας ἐπείγου καὶ πέραινε τὸ προκείμενον.

Step-by-Step Tactics for Resisting Pressure

*On Alcohol, Getting Called Chicken,
and Breaking Away*

[5] Since this illness is the cause of so many problems, therefore, we must try to get rid of it by exercises. We can start—as people practicing anything do—with little incidents that aren't too hard to face. For example,

- At a dinner party, someone raises a toast to you when you've had enough? Don't cave, and don't force yourself. Just put the glass down.
- Someone else asks you to gamble while you're drinking? Don't cave, and don't be afraid you'll get made fun of. Just do what Xenophanes did when Lasus of Hermione kept calling him a coward for not wanting to play dice with him: agree that you absolutely are a coward, and you lack the guts to risk getting shamed!
- Some windbag has latched onto you and won't let go? Don't cave. Just break away and get on with your business.

αἱ γὰρ τοιαῦται φυγαὶ καὶ διακρούσεις, ἐν ἐλαφραῖς μέμψεσι τὴν μελέτην ἔχουσαι τοῦ ἀδυσωπήτου, προεθίζουσιν ἡμᾶς ἐπὶ τὰ μείζονα.

καὶ τὸ τοῦ Δημοσθένους ἐνταῦθα καλῶς ἔχει διαμνημονεύειν· τῶν γὰρ Ἀθηναίων ὡρμημένων Ἁρπάλῳ βοηθεῖν καὶ κορυσσομένων ἐπὶ τὸν Ἀλέξανδρον ἐξαίφνης ἐπεφάνη Φιλόξενος ὁ τῶν ἐπὶ θαλάττῃ πραγμάτων Ἀλεξάνδρου στρατηγός. ἐκπλαγέντος δὲ τοῦ δήμου καὶ σιωπῶντος διὰ τὸν φόβον ὁ Δημοσθένης,

"τί ποιήσουσιν (ἔφη) τὸν ἥλιον ἰδόντες οἱ μὴ
    δυνάμενοι πρὸς λύχνον ἀντιβλέπειν;"

τί γὰρ ποιήσεις ἐν πράγμασι μεγάλοις, βασιλέως ἐντυγχάνοντος ἢ δήμου δυσωποῦντος, εἰ ποτήριον ἀπώσασθαι μὴ δύνασαι προτείνοντος συνήθους μηδὲ ἀδολέσχου λαβὴν διαφυγεῖν, ἀλλὰ παρέχεις ἐμπεριπατεῖν φλυάρῳ σαυτόν, οὐκ εὐτονῶν εἰπεῖν, "ὄψομαί σε αὖθις, νῦν δὲ οὐ σχολάζω";

[6] Καὶ μὴν οὐδ᾽ ἡ πρὸς τοὺς ἐπαίνους τοῦ ἀδυσωπήτου μελέτη καὶ ἄσκησις ἐν μικροῖς καὶ ἐλαφροῖς ἄχρηστός ἐστιν. οἷον ἐν συμποσίῳ φίλου κιθαρῳδὸς ᾄδει κακῶς ἢ πολλοῦ κωμῳδὸς ἐωνημένος ἐπιτρίβει

You see, escapes and refusals like these give us practice in resisting pressure at the cost of only slight offense, and they condition us for tougher cases.

On that note, it's good to recall a remark of Demosthenes. The Athenians were eager to aid Harpalus and were arming themselves against Alexander, when Philoxenus, Alexander's admiral, suddenly appeared. When the assembly was shocked and speechless in fear, Demosthenes quipped,

> "If they can't face a lamp, what'll they do when they see the sun?"

I mean, what will you do in great affairs—if a king comes asking, say, or an assembly's pressuring you—if you're unable to decline a glass offered by a friend or escape a windbag's clutches? If you'll instead let some blowhard walk all over you because you lack the nerve to say, "I'll catch you another time; I'm not free right now"?

Don't Join the Amen Corner

[6] And indeed, practice and training in resisting feelings of pressure in minor and trivial matters is of no small advantage when it comes to the pressure to join in praise. Say, for example, a performer sings badly at your friend's party, or some expensive actor

Μένανδρον, οἱ δὲ πολλοὶ κροτοῦσι καὶ θαυμάζουσιν·
οὐδὲν οἶμαι χαλεπὸν οὐδὲ δύσκολον ἀκούειν σιωπῇ
καὶ μὴ παρὰ τὸ φαινόμενον ἀνελευθέρως ἐπαινεῖν.

ἐὰν γὰρ ἐν τούτοις μὴ κρατῇς σαυτοῦ, τί ποιήσεις
φίλου ποίημα φαῦλον ἀναγινώσκοντος ἢ λόγον ἐπι-
δεικνυμένου γεγραμμένον ἀβελτέρως καὶ γελοίως;
ἐπαινέσεις δηλονότι καὶ συνεπιθορυβήσεις τοῖς κολακεύουσι. πῶς οὖν ἐν πράγμασιν ἁμαρτάνοντος
ἐπιλήψῃ; πῶς δὲ περὶ ἀρχὴν ἢ γάμον ἢ πολιτείαν
ἀγνωμονοῦντα νουθετήσεις;

ἐγὼ μὲν γὰρ οὐδὲ τὸ τοῦ Περικλέους ἀποδέχομαι
πρὸς τὸν ἀξιοῦντα μαρτυρίαν ψευδῆ μαρτυρῆσαι
φίλον, ᾧ προσῆν καὶ ὅρκος, εἰπόντος,

"μέχρι τοῦ βωμοῦ φίλος εἰμί"·

λίαν γὰρ ἐγγὺς ἦλθεν. ὁ δὲ πόρρωθεν ἑαυτὸν ἐθίσας
μήτε λέγοντος ἐπαινεῖν παρὰ γνώμην μήτε ᾄδοντος
κροτεῖν μήτε σκώπτοντος ἀφυῶς ἐπιγελᾶν οὐκ ἐάσει
μέχρι τούτου προελθεῖν οὐδ᾽ εἰπεῖν πρὸς τὸν ἐν ἐκείνοις ἀδυσώπητον "ὄμοσον ὑπὲρ ἐμοῦ καὶ τὰ ψευδῆ
μαρτύρησον" καὶ "ἀπόφηναι παρὰ τὸ δίκαιον."

he's hired flubs Menander . . . and the crowd claps and cheers. I don't think it's obnoxious or difficult to just listen in silence and not slavishly applaud in spite of the evidence.

I mean, if you don't control yourself in these matters, what will you do when a friend is reading you a bad poem or has you listen to him practicing some silly and absurd speech he's written? You'll presumably praise him and join his flatterers in hearty applause. Okay; but how will you correct him when he's making mistakes in real life? How will you talk sense to him when he's being unrealistic about running for office or getting married or making a policy decision?

Speaking for myself, I don't even accept the reply Pericles gave a friend who asked him to lie in court under oath—

"Up to the witness stand, I'm a friend."[19]

—because he got much too close. Whereas if you condition yourself not to praise a public speaker or clap for a performer or laugh at an unfunny joke despite yourself, you won't let things get to that point. If you're immune to pressure in those matters, you won't let anyone say to you, "swear and lie under oath for me" or "deliver a wrong verdict."

[7] Οὕτω δὲ δεῖ καὶ πρὸς τοὺς αἰτοῦντας ἀργύριον ἀνταίρειν, προεθιζόμενον ἐν τοῖς μήτε μεγάλοις μήτε δυσπαραιτήτοις. Ἀρχέλαος μὲν γὰρ ὁ τῶν Μακεδόνων βασιλεὺς παρὰ δεῖπνον αἰτηθεὶς ἔκπωμα χρυσοῦν ὑπ᾽ ἀνθρώπου μηδὲν ἡγουμένου καλὸν ἢ τὸ λαμβάνειν ἐκέλευσεν Εὐριπίδῃ τὸν παῖδα δοῦναι, καὶ πρὸς τὸν ἄνθρωπον ἐκεῖνον ἀποβλέψας,

"σὺ μέν (εἶπεν) αἰτεῖν ἐπιτήδειος εἶ καὶ μὴ λαμβάνειν,
οὗτος δὲ λαμβάνειν καὶ μὴ αἰτῶν,"

ἄριστα τοῦ διδόναι καὶ χαρίζεσθαι κύριον ποιῶν τὸ κρῖνον ἀλλὰ μὴ τὸ δυσωπούμενον· ἡμεῖς δὲ πολλάκις ἀνθρώπους ἐπιεικεῖς καὶ οἰκείους καὶ δεομένους περιορῶντες ἑτέροις αἰτοῦσιν ἐνδελεχῶς καὶ ἰταμῶς ἐδώκαμεν, οὐ δοῦναι θελήσαντες ἀλλ᾽ ἀρνήσασθαι μὴ δυνηθέντες. ὥσπερ Ἀντίγονος ὁ γέρων ὑπὸ Βίαντος ἐνοχληθεὶς πολλάκις,

"δότε (εἶπεν) "βίᾳ . . . τάλαντον καὶ ἀνάγκη."

The Dire Consequences of Caving

For Money

[7] This is also the way to oppose requests for money—that is, by developing the habit in cases which are unimportant and easy to refuse. For example, at a banquet, Archelaus, the king of Macedon, was asked for a golden goblet by a man whose top priority in life was getting things. Archelaus, though, told his slave to give it to Euripides, and looking at the man, said:

> "You're the one to ask and not receive; he's the one
> to receive even without asking."

He made his own judgment, not pressure, the deciding factor for his gifts and favors. It was very impressive.

You and I aren't like that, though; we often pass over worthy friends and relatives in distress and give money to others who nag and pester us—and not because we *want* to, but because we lack the strength to say no. A good example is what Antigonus, in his old age, said when Bias kept pestering him:

> "Oh, pay the man . . . this is a 'buy us' incident."[20]

καίτοι μάλιστα τῶν βασιλέων ἐμμελὴς ἦν καὶ πιθανὸς ἀποτρίβεσθαι τὰ τοιαῦτα. κυνικοῦ γάρ ποτε δραχμὴν αἰτήσαντος αὐτόν, "ἀλλ᾽ οὐ βασιλικόν," ἔφη, "τὸ δόμα"· τοῦ δὲ ὑποτυχόντος, "δός μοι τάλαντον," ἀπήντησεν,

"ἀλλ᾽ οὐ κυνικὸν τὸ λῆμμα."

Διογένης μὲν οὖν τοὺς ἀνδριάντας ᾔτει περιιὼν ἐν Κεραμεικῷ καὶ πρὸς τοὺς θαυμάζοντας ἔλεγεν ἀποτυγχάνειν μελετᾶν· ἡμῖν δὲ πρῶτον ἐμμελετητέον ἐστὶ τοῖς φαύλοις καὶ γυμναστέον περὶ τὰ μικρὰ πρὸς τὸ ἀρνεῖσθαι τοῖς αἰτοῦσιν οὐ προσηκόντως, ἵνα τοῖς προσηκόντως ληψομένοις ἐπικουρεῖν ἔχωμεν· οὐδεὶς γάρ, ὡς ὁ Δημοσθένης φησίν, εἰς ἃ μὴ δεῖ καταναλώσας τὰ παρόντα τῶν μὴ παρόντων εὐπορήσει πρὸς ἃ δεῖ. γίνεται δὲ ἡμῖν πολλαπλάσιον τὸ αἰσχρὸν ὅταν ἐλλίπωμεν εἰς τὰ καλὰ πλεονάσαντες τοῖς περιττοῖς.

[8] Ἐπεὶ δὲ οὐ χρημάτων μόνον ἡ δυσωπία κακὴ καὶ ἀγνώμων οἰκονόμος ἐστίν, ἀλλὰ καὶ περὶ τὰ μείζονα παραιρεῖται τὸ συμφέρον τοῦ λογισμοῦ

– (καὶ γὰρ ἰατρὸν νοσοῦντες οὐ παρακαλοῦμεν τὸν ἔμπειρον αἰσχυνόμενοι τὸν συνήθη, καὶ

And yet Antigonus had been the smoothest and most impressive of all the Hellenistic kings at deflecting such requests. When a Cynic wise man once asked him for fifty dollars, he replied, "That's not a gift that kings grant." When the man then rejoined, "Give me $250,000," he came back with, "That's not a gift that Cynics receive."[21]

Diogenes used to panhandle from statues in his neighborhood; he'd tell anyone who gawked that he was practicing getting turned down. Not us, though. We should practice on *irrelevant* people, and condition ourselves to refuse their trivial requests, if inappropriate. That way, we'll be able to meet appropriate requests—because (as Demosthenes says) if you spend all your money on what you don't need, then you'll never be able to spend money you *don't* have on what you *do* need. Besides, shame increases when we come up short for necessities because we've overspent on stupid stuff.

For Health, Education, Lawsuits,
and Personal Beliefs

[8] But dysopia isn't just a foolish and bad steward of money. It impacts our ability to weigh costs and benefits in more serious matters, too. For example:

– We're sick, but we don't call a specialist because we're ashamed not to go with our usual doctor.

27

– παισὶ διδασκάλους ἀντὶ τῶν χρηστῶν τοὺς
παρακαλοῦντας αἰρούμεθα,
– δίκην ἔχοντες πολλάκις οὐκ ἐῶμεν εἰπεῖν τὸν
ὠφέλιμον καὶ ἀγοραῖον, ἀλλ᾽ οἰκείου τινὸς
ἢ συγγενοῦς υἱῷ χαριζόμενοι παρεδώκαμεν
ἐμπανηγυρίσαι, καὶ
– τέλος δὲ πολλούς ἐστιν ἰδεῖν καὶ τῶν φιλοσο-
φεῖν λεγομένων Ἐπικουρείους καὶ Στωϊκοὺς
ὄντας, οὐχ ἑλομένους οὐδὲ κρίναντας ἀλλὰ
προσθεμένους δυσωποῦσιν οἰκείοις καὶ
φίλοις)

φέρε δὴ καὶ πρὸς ταῦτα πόρρωθεν ἐν τοῖς ἐπιτυχοῦσι
καὶ μικροῖς γυμνάζωμεν ἑαυτούς, ἐθίζοντες μήτε
κουρεῖ μήτε γναφεῖ κατὰ δυσωπίαν χρῆσθαι μηδὲ
καταλύειν ἐν φαύλῳ πανδοκείῳ βελτίονος παρόντος
ὅτι πολλάκις ὁ πανδοκεὺς ἠσπάσατο ἡμᾶς,

ἀλλ᾽ ἔθους ἕνεκα, κἂν ᾖ παρὰ μικρόν, αἱρεῖσθαι
τὸ βέλτιον, ὥσπερ οἱ Πυθαγορικοὶ παρεφύλαττον ἀεὶ
μηδέποτε τῷ δεξιῷ μηρῷ τὸν εὐώνυμον ἐπιτιθέναι
μηδὲ τὸν ἄρτιον ἀντὶ τοῦ περιττοῦ λαβεῖν τῶν ἄλλων
ἐπ᾽ ἴσης ἐχόντων.

- Instead of choosing the best teachers for our children, we choose those who ask for the job.
- We often won't let the best and most skilled lawyer represent us in a lawsuit. Instead, we'll hand our case off to the son of some friend or relative to help his career.
- Worst of all is seeing all the "philosophers" who are Epicureans and Stoics not by choice or conviction, but because they've caved to pressure from friends and relatives!

Please. Long before we reach that point, let's train for those situations in small, everyday encounters. Let's make a habit of not patronizing a barber or cleaners as dysopia dictates, and of not staying in a crummy hotel when there is a better one available simply because the owner says hello to us.

The General Rule: Always Choose the Better Option

Instead, for the practice, let's make a habit of *choosing the better option even when the difference is negligible*, much as Pythagoreans made a point of never resting their left leg on their right, and of picking, when all else was equal, an even number rather than an odd.

ἐθιστέον δὲ καὶ θυσίαν ποιούμενον ἢ γάμον ἤ τινα ἄλλην τοιαύτην ὑποδοχὴν μὴ τὸν ἀσπασάμενον καλεῖν ἢ προσδραμόντα μᾶλλον ἢ τὸν εὔνουν καὶ χρηστόν· ὁ γὰρ οὕτως ἐθισθεὶς καὶ ἀσκήσας δυσάλωτος ἔσται, μᾶλλον δὲ ὅλως ἀνεπιχείρητος, ἐν τοῖς μείζοσι.

[9] Περὶ μὲν οὖν ἀσκήσεως ἱκανὰ καὶ ταῦτα· τῶν δὲ χρησίμων ἐπιλογισμῶν . . .

. . . πρῶτός ἐστιν ὁ διδάσκων καὶ ὑπομιμνήσκων ὅτι πᾶσι μὲν τοῖς πάθεσιν ἀκολουθεῖ καὶ τοῖς νοσήμασιν ἃ φεύγειν δι᾽ αὐτῶν δοκοῦμεν· ἀδοξίαι φιλοδοξίαις καὶ λῦπαι φιληδονίαις καὶ πόνοι μαλακίαις καὶ φιλονικίαις ἧτται καὶ καταδίκαι·

τῇ δὲ δυσωπίᾳ συμβέβηκεν ἀτεχνῶς φευγούσῃ καπνὸν ἀδοξίας εἰς πῦρ ἐμβάλλειν ἑαυτήν. αἰσχυνόμενοι γὰρ ἀντιλέγειν τοῖς ἀγνωμόνως δυσωποῦσιν ὕστερον δυσωποῦνται τοὺς δικαίως ἐγκαλοῦντας, καὶ

Also, if we're going to host a feast or wedding or some other such reception, we should make a habit of not just inviting any random person who says hello or runs over to meet us. We should only invite kind and well-intentioned people.

If you train and develop these habits, you see, you'll be hard to victimize—indeed, you'll be utterly impervious to pressure—in more serious situations.

[9] Enough about training; now for useful reflections.

Ten Useful Reflections

1. Caving Exacerbates Problems Rather Than Solving Them

The first reflection teaches and reminds us that all problematic emotions and pathologies lead to the very problems we think we're escaping through them: ambition leads to disgrace, bingeing to grief, laziness to more work, litigiousness to defeat and loss in court.[22]

Just so dysopia, in scrambling to escape the smoke of disgrace, jumps into the fire. You see, when people feel too ashamed to say no to bullying, they later feel bullied when they're duly called out

δεδιότες μέμψιν ἐλαφρὰν πολλάκις αἰσχύνην ὁμολο-
γουμένην ὑπομένουσιν·

- καὶ γὰρ αἰτοῦντος ἀργύριον φίλου δυσωπηθέ-
ντες ἀντειπεῖν οὐκ ἔχοντες ἀσχημονοῦσι μετ᾽
ὀλίγον ἐξελεγχόμενοι,
- καὶ βοηθήσειν ὁμολογήσαντες ἐνίοις δίκην
ἔχουσιν, εἶτα τοὺς ἑτέρους διατραπέντες ἀπο-
κρύπτονται καὶ δραπετεύουσι.
- πολλοὺς δὲ καὶ περὶ γάμου θυγατρὸς ἢ
ἀδελφῆς εἰς ὁμολογίαν ἀλυσιτελῆ κατακλεί-
σασα δυσωπία ψεύδεσθαι πάλιν ἀναγκάζει
μετατιθεμένους.

[10] Ὁ μὲν γὰρ εἰπὼν ὅτι πάντες οἱ τὴν Ἀσίαν κατοι-
κοῦντες ἑνὶ δουλεύουσιν ἀνθρώπῳ διὰ τὸ μὴ δύνασθαι μίαν εἰπεῖν τὴν οὐκ συλλαβὴν οὐκ ἐσπούδασεν
ἀλλ᾽ ἔσκωψεν· τοῖς δὲ δυσωπουμένοις, κἂν μηδὲν εἴ-
πωσιν, ἔξεστιν ὀφρῦν ἐπάρασι μόνον ἢ κάτω κύψασι
πολλὰς ἀβουλήτους καὶ ἀτόπους ὑπουργίας διαφεύ-
γειν· τὴν γὰρ σιωπὴν ὁ μὲν Εὐριπίδης φησὶ τοῖς σο-
φοῖς ἀπόκρισιν εἶναι, κινδυνεύομεν δὲ μᾶλλον αὐτῆς
δεῖσθαι πρὸς τοὺς ἀγνώμονας, ἐπεὶ τοὺς χαρίεντας
ἔστι καὶ παρηγορῆσαι.

on it—and for fearing a little criticism, they face a full-on shaming. Consider:

- When people are bullied into granting a friend's request for money they don't have, they soon get exposed and disgraced.[23]
- When people agree to help one side in a lawsuit, they can't bear to face the other, so they hide and slink away.
- After dysopia pressures men into making a foolish agreement for a daughter's or sister's marriage, it then compels many of them to break their word and make new arrangements.

2. Silence Is an Effective Answer to an Improper Request

[10] It was only a joke—no more—when a man once said that all the inhabitants of the Middle East were enslaved to a single human being because they couldn't say the one syllable "no."[24] Still, when you're feeling bullied, you really can—without saying a word—simply raise or lower an eyebrow to avoid doing many irritating and off-putting jobs. (Euripides does say that "silence is an answer to the wise," but in reality, we're probably going to need silence more for dealing with unreasonable people, since normal people can be reasoned with.)

Καὶ πρόχειρά γε δεῖ καὶ συχνὰ τῶν ἐπιφανῶν καὶ ἀγαθῶν ἀνδρῶν ἔχειν ἀποφθέγματα καὶ μνημονεύειν πρὸς τοὺς δυσωποῦντας· οἷον τὸ Φωκίωνος πρὸς Ἀντίπατρον·

"οὐ δύνασαί μοι καὶ φίλῳ χρῆσθαι καὶ κόλακι."

καὶ πρὸς τοὺς Ἀθηναίους ἐπιδοῦναι κελεύοντας αὐτὸν ἐν ἑορτῇ καὶ κροτοῦντας,

"αἰσχύνομαι (εἶπεν) ὑμῖν **ἐπι**διδοὺς τούτῳ δὲ μὴ **ἀπο**διδούς,"

Καλλικλέα δείξας τὸν δανειστήν.
"πενίαν" γὰρ "οὐχ ὁμολογεῖν αἰσχρόν," ὡς Θουκυδίδης φησίν, "ἀλλ᾽ ἔργῳ μὴ διαφεύγειν αἴσχιον." ὁ δὲ ἀβελτερίᾳ καὶ μαλακίᾳ πρὸς τὸν αἰτοῦντα δυσωπούμενος εἰπεῖν

οὐκ ἔστ᾽ ἐν ἄντροις λευκός, ὦ ξέν᾽, ἄργυρος,

εἶτα ὥσπερ ἐνέχυρον προέμενος τὴν ἐπαγγελίαν

3. *Quote Famous Sayings and Quips to Soften Your Refusal*

It's also important to have a good supply of go-to sayings from famous authorities and to quote them to bullies. For example, there's Phocion's remark to Antipater:

> "You cannot have me as both your friend and flatterer."

There's also what Phocion told the Athenians at a festival. As they were clapping and cheering for him, they clamored for him to help defray their expenses. Phocion pointed at Callicles the moneylender and quipped:

> "I'd be ashamed to defray *you* till I repay *him*!"

You see, it's as Thucydides says [2.40.1, Pericles speaking]: "Owning up to poverty isn't shameful; true shame lies in failing to avoid it." Whereas a wimp who feels too bullied to tell a petitioner,

> Forsooth, no silver in this cave, my friend!

and instead just blurts out a promise to help,

αἰδοῦς ἀχαλκεύτοισιν ἔζευκται πέδαις.

ὁ δὲ Περσαῖος ἀργύριόν τινι τῶν γνωρίμων δανείζων δι᾽ ἀγορᾶς καὶ τραπέζης ἐποιεῖτο τὸ συμβόλαιον μεμνημένος δηλονότι τοῦ Ἡσιόδου λέγοντος

καί τε κασιγνήτῳ γελάσας ἐπὶ μάρτυρα θέσθαι

θαυμάσαντος δὲ ἐκείνου καὶ εἰπόντος, "οὕτως, ὦ Περσαῖε, νομικῶς;" "ναί," εἶπεν,

"ἵνα φιλικῶς ἀπολάβω καὶ μὴ νομικῶς ἀπαιτήσω."

πολλοὶ γὰρ ἐν ἀρχῇ διὰ δυσωπίαν προέμενοι τὸ πιστὸν ὕστερον ἐχρήσαντο τοῖς νομίμοις μετ᾽ ἔχθρας.

[11] πάλιν ὁ Πλάτων Ἑλίκωνι τῷ Κυζικηνῷ διδοὺς πρὸς Διονύσιον ἐπιστολὴν ἐπήνεσεν αὐτὸν ὡς ἐπιεικῆ καὶ μέτριον, εἶτα προσέγραψε τῇ ἐπιστολῇ τελευτώσῃ·

is bound by chains which shame, not man, hath
made.[25]

When [the Stoic wise man] Persaeus lent money to
a man he knew, he had a contract drawn up by a
banker downtown. He was obviously thinking of
Hesiod's line [*Works and Days* 371]:

Even with your brother, laugh—and get a witness.

When the man was surprised and asked, "So legal-
istic, Persaeus!?" "Yes," replied Persaeus,

"To make sure the money comes back on good
terms—not contractual terms."

You see, many who forgo an IOU at the outset
because of dysopia later resort to the law—and wind
up hated for it.

4. *Employ Irony as Needed When Offering a Recommendation*

[11] Plato wrote Dionysius a letter of recommendation for Helicon of Cyzicus. In it, he praised
the man as moderate and reasonable, but added
at the end:

"γράφω δέ σοι ταῦτα περὶ ἀνθρώπου, ζῴου φύσει
εὐμεταβόλου."

Ξενοκράτης δὲ καίπερ αὐστηρὸς ὢν τὸν τρόπον ὅμως
ὑπὸ δυσωπίας ἐκάμφθη καὶ συνέστησε Πολυπέρχο-
ντι δι᾽ ἐπιστολῆς ἄνθρωπον οὐ χρηστόν, ὡς τὸ ἔργον
ἔδειξεν· δεξιωσαμένου δὲ αὐτὸν τοῦ Μακεδόνος καὶ
πυθομένου μή τινος ἔχοι χρείαν, ᾔτησε τάλαντον· ὁ
δὲ ἐκείνῳ μὲν ἔδωκε Ξενοκράτει δὲ ἔγραψε παραινῶν
ἐπιμελέστερον τὸ λοιπὸν ἐξετάζειν οὓς συνίστησιν.
   ὁ μὲν οὖν Ξενοκράτης ἠγνόησεν· ἡμεῖς δὲ καὶ πάνυ
πολλάκις ἐπιστάμενοι τοὺς πονηροὺς καὶ γράμματα
προϊέμεθα καὶ χρήματα, βλάπτοντες ἑαυτοὺς οὐ μεθ᾽
ἡδονῆς ὥσπερ οἱ ταῖς ἑταίραις χαριζόμενοι καὶ τοῖς
κόλαξιν, ἀλλὰ δυσχεραίνοντες καὶ βαρυνόμενοι τὴν
ἀναίδειαν ἀνατρέπουσαν ἡμῶν καὶ καταβιαζομένην
τὸν λογισμόν. εἰ γὰρ πρὸς ἄλλο τι, καὶ πρὸς τοὺς δυ-
σωποῦντας ἔξεστιν εἰπεῖν τό

   μανθάνω μὲν οἷα δρᾶν μέλλω κακά

τὰ ψευδῆ μαρτυρῶν ἢ τα μὴ δίκαια κρίνων ἢ τὰ μὴ
συμφέροντα χειροτονῶν ἢ δανειζόμενος ὑπὲρ τοῦ
μὴ ἀποδώσοντος.

"I'm writing all this about a human being—a creature prone to change."

Xenocrates was a strict man, but he caved to dysopia
anyway and wrote Polyperchon a letter of introduction for a man who was a scumbag—as the event
showed. When the Macedonian welcomed him and
inquired if he needed anything, the man requested
$250,000. Polyperchon gave him the money, but he
wrote Xenocrates and advised him to scrutinize the
people he recommended more carefully in the future.

Now, Xenocrates didn't know any better, but
all too often you and I dispatch letters of recommendation and money, and we're fully aware their
recipients don't deserve it. We harm ourselves, but
we don't get any of the pleasure that patrons of
prostitutes and flatterers do. No, we're disgusted;
we *resent* their shameless asking, which unsettles
and conquers our reason. I mean, if it's ever appropriate to say so, then we can certainly say to our
bullies [Euripides, *Medea* 1078],

I know what I'm about to do is bad.

We can say that as we're telling lies under oath, or
rendering an unjust verdict, or voting for a stupid
policy, or borrowing money for someone who
won't pay it back.

39

[12] Διὸ τῶν παθῶν μάλιστα τῷ δυσωπεῖσθαι τὸ μετανοεῖν οὐχ ὕστερον, ἀλλ᾽ εὐθὺς ἐν οἷς πράττει πάρεστι· καὶ γὰρ διδόντες ἀχθόμεθα καὶ μαρτυροῦντες αἰσχυνόμεθα καὶ συνεργοῦντες ἀδοξοῦμεν καὶ μὴ παρέχοντες ἐλεγχόμεθα. πολλὰ γὰρ ὑπ᾽ ἀσθενείας τοῦ ἀντιλέγειν καὶ τῶν ἀδυνάτων ἡμῖν ὑπισχνούμεθα τοῖς λιπαροῦσιν, ὡς συστάσεις ἐν αὐλαῖς καὶ πρὸς ἡγεμόνας ἐντεύξεις, μὴ βουλόμενοι μηδὲ εὐτονοῦντες εἰπεῖν· "οὐκ οἶδεν ἡμᾶς ὁ βασιλεύς, ἀλλ᾽ ἑτέρους ὅρα μᾶλλον"·

ὡς Λύσανδρος Ἀγησιλάῳ προσκεκρουκὼς ἀξιούμενος δὲ μέγιστον δύνασθαι παρ᾽ αὐτῷ διὰ τὴν δόξαν οὐκ ᾐσχύνετο παραιτεῖσθαι τοὺς ἐντυγχάνοντας, ἀπιέναι πρὸς ἑτέρους κελεύων καὶ πειρᾶσθαι τῶν μᾶλλον αὐτοῦ παρὰ τῷ βασιλεῖ δυναμένων.

οὐ γὰρ αἰσχρὸν τὸ μὴ πάντα δύνασθαι· τὸ δὲ μὴ δυναμένους ἢ μὴ πεφυκότας ἀναδέχεσθαι τὰ τοιαῦτα καὶ παραβιάζεσθαι πρὸς τῷ αἰσχρῷ λυπηρότατόν ἐστιν.

5. Regret Is Instantaneous, So Swallow Your (False) Pride

Plutarch now talks about our stupid tendency to promise audiences with kings and princes—a principle that is just as applicable to the c-suite.

[12] And so it is that with dysopia, more than any other emotion, regret appears not later, but simultaneously with the very act of caving.[26] I mean, in giving, we're aggravated; in testifying, ashamed; in helping out, we're vilified; and if we don't deliver, we're unmasked. In lacking the strength to say no, we promise our importuners many things we can't make good on—an audience with the palace, say, or introductions to leaders. We can't bring ourselves to say, "The king doesn't know me; you'll have to ask someone else."

Lysander is the model. After he fell from Agesilaus's favor, he was still thought to have major influence with him by virtue of his popularity. Nevertheless, he wasn't ashamed to turn requests down and tell those who inquired to go and try asking others who had greater influence with the king.

You see, there's no shame in being unable to do everything. When you lack the power and the temperament, though, agreeing to those kinds of requests—and forcing them—adds a world of grief to shame.

[13] Ἀπ᾽ ἄλλης δὲ ἀρχῆς· τὰ μὲν μέτρια καὶ πρέποντα δεῖ προθύμως ὑπουργεῖν τοῖς ἀξιοῦσι μὴ δυσωπουμένους ἀλλ᾽ ἑκόντας, ἐν δὲ τοῖς βλαβεροῖς καὶ ἀτόποις τὸ τοῦ Ζήνωνος ἀεὶ πρόχειρον ἔχειν, ὃς ἀπαντήσας νεανίσκῳ τινὶ τῶν συνήθων παρὰ τὸ τεῖχος ἡσυχῇ βαδίζοντι καὶ πυθόμενος ὅτι φεύγει φίλον ἀξιοῦντα μαρτυρεῖν αὐτῷ τὰ ψευδῆ, "τί λέγεις," φησίν, "ἀβέλτερε;"

"σὲ μὲν ἐκεῖνος ἀγνωμονῶν καὶ ἀδικῶν οὐ δέδιεν οὐδὲ αἰσχύνεται, σὺ δὲ ἐκεῖνον ὑπὲρ τῶν δικαίων οὐ θαρρεῖς ὑποστῆναι;"

ὁ μὲν γὰρ εἰπών

ποτὶ πονηρὸν οὐκ ἄχρηστον ὅπλον ἁ πονηρία

—κακῶς ἐθίζει μιμούμενον ἀμύνεσθαι τὴν κακίαν, τὸ δὲ τοὺς ἀναιδῶς καὶ ἀδυσωπήτως ἐνοχλοῦντας ἀποτρίβεσθαι τῷ ἀδυσωπήτῳ, καὶ μὴ χαρίζεσθαι τὰ αἰσχρὰ τοῖς ἀναισχύντοις αἰσχυνόμενον, ὀρθῶς καὶ δικαίως γινόμενόν ἐστιν ὑπὸ τῶν νοῦν ἐχόντων.

[13] Here's another way to look at it: we should comply with reasonable and appropriate requests readily, not because we feel pressured to, but gladly. With harmful and improper requests, though, we should be ever ready to quote Zeno. One day he came across a young man he knew pacing up and down by the city wall. When he discovered that the young man was avoiding a friend who'd asked him to lie in court, he said, "Wait a minute, silly:

"He's being inappropriate and wrong to you, and he's not afraid or ashamed of it. . . . Don't you have the courage to stand up to *him* for what's right?"

You see, the man who said—

Against a villain, a not-bad weapon's villainy

—tells us to resist bad behavior by imitating it. That's bad advice. No, *the way to get rid of bullies who shamelessly pressure us is by being impervious to pressure ourselves*. It's *not* to get shamed into granting shameless people shameful requests. *That* is what reasonable people rightly and justly do.

[14] Ἔτι τοίνυν τῶν δυσωπούντων τοῖς μὲν ἀδόξοις
καὶ ταπεινοῖς καὶ μηδενὸς ἀξίοις οὐ μέγα ἔργον ἀντι-
σχεῖν, ἀλλὰ καὶ μετὰ γέλωτος ἔνιοι καὶ σκώμματος ἐκ-
κλίνουσι τοὺς τοιούτους, ὡς Θεόκριτος, δυεῖν αὐτὸν
ἐν βαλανείῳ στλεγγίδα κιχραμένων, τοῦ μὲν ξένου,
τοῦ δὲ γνωρίμου κλέπτου, μετὰ παιδιᾶς ἀμφοτέρους
διεκρούσατο εἰπών,

"σὲ μὲν οὐκ οἶδα, σὲ δὲ οἶδα."

Λυσιμάχῃ δὲ Ἀθήνησιν, ἡ τῆς Πολιάδος ἱέρεια, τῶν τὰ
ἱερὰ προσαγαγόντων ὀρεωκόμων ἐγχέαι κελευόντων,

"ἀλλ᾽ ὀκνῶ (εἶπεν) μὴ καὶ τοῦτο πάτριον γένηται."

καὶ Ἀντίγονος πρός τινα νεανίσκον γεγονότα μὲν ἐκ
λοχαγοῦ χαρίεντος, αὐτὸν δ᾽ ἄτολμον ὄντα καὶ μα-
λακόν, ἀξιοῦντα δὲ προαχθῆναι,

"παρ᾽ ἐμοί (φησιν), ὦ μειράκιον, ἀνδραγαθίας εἰσὶν
οὐ πατραγαθίας τιμαί."

6. *Use Humor to Decline an Inappropriate Request from Below*

[14] Moreover, when our bullies are unimportant nobodies, it takes no great effort to resist them; some turn such types away with a joke and a laugh. For example,

- In the public baths a couple of guys—one a stranger, the other a notorious thief—wanted to borrow Theocritus's body groomer. He used humor to get rid of both, quipping:
  "You, I don't know; you, I do."[27]
- Lysimache was a priestess in Athens. When some deliverymen brought the sacramental wine and chalices and asked her to pour them a "libation," she quipped,
  "Sorry, boys, can't risk making a 'customary observance' of it."
- A young man was the son of a distinguished military officer, but unimpressive himself. When he asked for a promotion, Antigonus told him,
  "Around here, kid, we recognize attitude, not dad-itude."

[15] Καὶ μὴν ἐάνπερ ὁ δυσωπῶν ἔνδοξος ᾖ καὶ δυνατός (οἳ δὴ μάλιστα καὶ δυσπαραίτητοι καὶ δυσαπότριπτοι περὶ τὰς κρίσεις καὶ τὰς χειροτονίας ἐντυγχάνοντές εἰσιν), ὃ μὲν ἔπραξεν ὁ Κάτων νέος ὢν ἔτι πρὸς Κάτλον οὐκ ἄν τινι φανείη ῥᾴδιον ἴσως οὐδ᾽ ἀναγκαῖον.

ὁ γὰρ Κάτλος ἦν μὲν ἐν ἀξιώματι τῶν Ῥωμαίων μεγίστῳ καὶ τότε τὴν τιμητικὴν ἀρχὴν εἶχεν· ἀνέβη δὲ πρὸς τὸν Κάτωνα τεταγμένον ἐπὶ τοῦ δημοσίου ταμιείου παραιτησόμενός τινα τῶν ἐζημιωμένων ὑπ᾽ αὐτοῦ καὶ λιπαρὴς ἐγίνετο ταῖς δεήσεσι προσβιαζόμενος, ἄχρι οὗ δυσανασχετήσας ἐκεῖνος,

"αἰσχρόν ἐστιν (ἔφη), Κάτλε, σὲ τὸν τιμητὴν ἀπαλλαγῆναι μὴ βουλόμενον ἐντεῦθεν ὑπὸ τῶν ἐμῶν ὑπηρετῶν ἕλκεσθαι"·

καὶ ὁ Κάτλος αἰσχυνθεὶς πρὸς ὀργὴν ἀπῆλθεν.

σκόπει δὲ μὴ τὸ τοῦ Ἀγησιλάου καὶ τὸ τοῦ Θεμιστοκλέους ἐπιεικέστερόν ἐστι καὶ μετριώτερον. ὁ μὲν γὰρ

7. Guilt-Trip an Inappropriate Request
from Above

[15] Sometimes, though, your bully is famous or powerful—and such types are, without a doubt, the hardest to refuse and get rid of when they come asking about a decision or expression of support. When that happens, the reply that [the Younger] Cato (who was still young at the time) made to Catulus will probably seem neither easy nor necessary.

You see, Catulus was held in the highest regard by the Romans—indeed, he was Censor at the time. Cato, meanwhile, was in charge of public finances, and Catulus came to ask him about getting a man out of a fine he'd issued. Catulus began harassing and importuning him until Cato finally lost it and said,

> "It's shameful, Catulus, that you—the Censor!—won't leave, which means my staff will be dragging you out."

Catulus was shamed out of it and went off in anger.

Consider instead whether these responses by Agesilaus and Themistocles are more appropriate and reasonable. When Agesilaus was told by his father

Ἀγησίλαος ὑπὸ τοῦ πατρὸς κελευόμενος κρῖναί τινα δίκην παρὰ τὸν νόμον,

"ἀλλ᾽ ὑπὸ σοῦ (ἔφη), πάτερ, πείθεσθαι τοῖς νόμοις ἐδιδασκόμην ἀπ᾽ ἀρχῆς· διὸ καὶ νῦν σοι πείθομαι μηδὲν ποιεῖν παράνομον."

ὁ δὲ Θεμιστοκλῆς πρὸς τὸν Σιμωνίδην ἀξιοῦντά τι τῶν μὴ δικαίων,

"οὔτ᾽ ἂν σὺ ποιητὴς ἀγαθὸς εἴης (ἔφη), παρὰ μέλος ᾄδων οὔτ᾽ ἂν ἐγὼ χρηστὸς ἄρχων παρὰ νόμον κρίνων."

[16] καίτοι οὐ διὰ τὴν τοῦ ποδὸς πρὸς τὴν λύραν ἀμετρίαν, ὡς Πλάτων ἔλεγε, καὶ πόλεις πόλεσι καὶ φίλοι φίλοις διαφερόμενοι τὰ ἔσχατα δρῶσί τε καὶ πάσχουσιν, ἀλλὰ διὰ τὴν περὶ τὰ νόμιμα καὶ δίκαια πλημμέλειαν.

ἀλλ᾽ ὅμως ἔνιοι τὴν ἐν μέλεσι καὶ γράμμασι καὶ μέτροις ἀκρίβειαν αὐτοὶ φυλάττοντες ἑτέρους ἐν ἀρχαῖς καὶ κρίσεσι καὶ πράξεσιν ἀξιοῦσιν ὀλιγωρεῖν τοῦ καλῶς ἔχοντος. διὸ καὶ τούτῳ μάλιστα χρηστέον πρὸς αὑτούς.

— ἐντυγχάνει σοι δικάζοντι ῥήτωρ ἢ βουλεύοντι

to decide a case in a way that went contrary to the law, he replied,

> "But Father, you were the one who first taught me to obey the law, so I'll obey you now too and do nothing contrary to the law."

And when Simonides asked Themistocles for some improper exception, he replied,

> "You wouldn't be much of a poet if your singing violated the music, and I wouldn't be much of a judge if my decisions violated the law."

[16] Yet cities don't turn against cities or friends against friends and commit and suffer atrocities all because words and music get out of sync, as Plato used to say [in *Clitophon* 407c–d]. No, they do that because of clamorous mistakes in matters of justice and law.

Still, some who are sticklers themselves about melody and words and rhythm expect others to ignore propriety in their leadership roles and decisions and dealings. *That*, therefore, is the very weapon we must use against them:

> – Say a lawyer asks a "favor" when you're trying a case, or you're a senator and it's some

δημαγωγός· ὁμολόγησον ἐὰν ἐκεῖνος σολοικίσῃ
προοιμιαζόμενος ἢ βαρβαρίσῃ διηγούμενος·
οὐ γὰρ ἐθελήσει διὰ τὸ φαινόμενον αἰσχρόν·
ἐνίους γοῦν ὁρῶμεν οὐδὲ φωνήεντι συγκροῦ-
σαι φωνῆεν ἐν τῷ λέγειν ὑπομένοντας.
– ἕτερον πάλιν δυσωποῦντα τῶν ἐπιφανῶν καὶ
ἐνδόξων κέλευσον ὀρχούμενον δι᾽ ἀγορᾶς δι-
εξελθεῖν ἢ διαστρέψαντα τὸ πρόσωπον· ἐὰν δὲ
ἀρνῆται, σός ἐστιν ὁ καιρὸς εἰπεῖν καὶ πυθέσθαι
τί αἰσχρόν ἐστιν, τὸ σολοικίσαι καὶ διαστρέψαι
τὸ πρόσωπον ἢ τὸ λῦσαι τὸν νόμον καὶ παραβῆ-
ναι τὸν ὅρκον καὶ πλέον νεῖμαι τῷ πονηρῷ τοῦ
ἀγαθοῦ παρὰ τὸ δίκαιον.

ἔτι τοίνυν, ὥσπερ Νικόστρατος ὁ Ἀργεῖος Ἀρχιδάμου
παρακαλοῦντος αὐτὸν ἐπὶ χρήμασι πολλοῖς καὶ γάμῳ
γυναικὸς ᾧ βούλεται Λακαίνης προδοῦναι Κρῶμνον
οὐκ ἔφη γεγονέναι τὸν Ἀρχίδαμον ἀφ᾽ Ἡρακλέους·
ἐκεῖνον μὲν γὰρ ἀποκτιννύναι περιιόντα τοὺς πονη-
ρούς, τοῦτον δὲ τοὺς χρηστοὺς ποιεῖν πονηρούς·
οὕτω καὶ ἡμῖν πρὸς ἄνθρωπον ἀξιοῦντα καλὸν κἀ-
γαθὸν λέγεσθαι ῥητέον, ἂν βιάζηται καὶ δυσωπῇ, μὴ
πρέποντα ποιεῖν μηδὲ ἄξια τῆς περὶ αὐτὸν εὐγενείας
καὶ ἀρετῆς.

activist. Tell 'em you'll do it if *he*'ll agree to make a blatant grammatical mistake in a big public speech. He won't, you see, because of "the shame." (Indeed, some people can't even stand having one vowel come after another when they speak![28])

– Or say it's some prominent and respected person pressuring you. Tell him to go through the town square sashaying or making a funny face. If he won't, that's the perfect time for you to pipe up and ask him what's really "shameful": a grammatical mistake or funny face? Or breaking the law, violating an oath, and unethically favoring a bad man over a good one?

When Archidamus offered Nicostratus of Argos money and a bride of his choice to betray the city of Cromnum, Nicostratus replied that Archidamus was no true descendant of Hercules. Hercules, he explained, had slain evildoers, whereas Archidamus here was trying to turn good men into doers of evil.

In the same way, if a person bullies and pressures us but still expects to be called a gentleman, we must tell him that his behavior is improper and unworthy of his birth and stature.

[17] Ἐπὶ δὲ τῶν φαύλων ὁρᾶν χρὴ καὶ διανοεῖσθαι

– τὸν φιλάργυρον εἰ δυσωπήσεις ἄνευ συμβο-
λαίου δανεῖσαι τάλαντον ἢ
– τὸν φιλότιμον ἐκστῆναι τῆς προεδρίας ἢ
– τὸν φίλαρχον τῆς παραγγελίας ἐπίδοξον ὄντα
κρατήσειν.

δεινὸν γὰρ ἂν ἀληθῶς φανείη τούτους μὲν ἐν νο-
σήμασι καὶ παθήμασιν ἀκάμπτους διαμένειν καὶ ἐχυ-
ροὺς καὶ δυσμεταθέτους, ἡμᾶς δὲ βουλομένους καὶ
φάσκοντας εἶναι φιλοκάλους καὶ φιλοδικαίους μὴ
κρατεῖν ἑαυτῶν ἀλλ᾽ ἀνατρέπεσθαι καὶ προΐεσθαι
τὴν ἀρετήν.
καὶ γὰρ εἰ μὲν οἱ δυσωποῦντες ἐπὶ δόξῃ καὶ δυνά-
μει τοῦτο ποιοῦσιν ἄτοπόν ἐστι κοσμοῦντας ἑτέρους
καὶ αὔξοντας ἀσχημονεῖν αὐτοὺς καὶ κακῶς ἀκούειν,
ὥσπερ οἱ παραβραβεύοντες ἐν τοῖς ἀγῶσι καὶ περὶ
τὰς χειροτονίας ἐξ οὗ προσηκόντων ἀρχεῖα καὶ στε-
φάνους ἄλλοις χαριζόμενοι καὶ δόξαν ἀφαιροῦνται τὸ
ἔνδοξον αὐτῶν καὶ τὸ καλόν·
εἰ δὲ χρημάτων ἕνεκα προσκείμενον ὁρῶμεν τὸν
δυσωποῦντα, πῶς οὐ παρίσταται δεινὸν εἶναι τὸ τῆς
ἰδίας δόξης καὶ ἀρετῆς ἀφειδεῖν ἵνα τὸ τοῦ δεῖνος βαλ-
λάντιον βαρύτερον γένηται; καίτοι παρίσταταί γε τοῖς

8. *Addicts Show Us What* True *Resistance to Pressure Looks Like*

[17] Look at people whose brains are addled, and ask yourself—*could* you pressure a person addicted to:

- *money* to loan you $5,000 without a note?
- *status* to give up their perks?
- *power* to quit a race they'll probably win?[29]

Doesn't it seem strange that these disordered and pathological types remain so stubborn and unbending and resolute, while you and I—who want to be and who go around saying that we're obsessed with propriety and justice—*we* panic, and instead of controlling ourselves, throw our integrity away?

Because, you see, if our bullies do what they do for popularity and power, it makes no sense to make *other* people look good or great by disgracing ourselves and getting a bad name. That's what corrupt officials do in sports and with appointments: they award government jobs and prizes and recognition to others not based on merit, and so rob themselves of their own reputation and honor.[30]

However, if we see that the bully pressuring us is motivated by money, then how can we fail to realize that it's bizarre to ruin our own reputation and integrity merely to fatten some other person's wallet?

πολλοῖς τὰ τοιαῦτα καὶ οὐ λανθάνουσιν ἑαυτοὺς ἐξα-
μαρτάνοντες, ὥσπερ οἱ τὰς μεγάλας κύλικας ἐκπίνειν
ἀναγκαζόμενοι μόλις καὶ στένοντες καὶ τὰ πρόσωπα
διαστρέψαντες ἐκτελοῦσι τὸ προστεταγμένον.

[18] ἀλλ᾽ ἔοικεν ἡ τῆς ψυχῆς ἀτονία σώματος κράσει
καὶ πρὸς ἀλέαν κακῶς πεφυκυίᾳ καὶ πρὸς κρύος· ἐπαι-
νούμενοί τε γὰρ ὑπὸ τῶν δυσωπούντων παντάπασι
θρύπτονται καὶ χαλῶνται, πρός τε τὰς μέμψεις καὶ
ὑφοράσεις τῶν ἀποτυγχανόντων ψοφοδεῶς καὶ δει-
λῶς ἔχουσι. δεῖ δὲ ἀντισχυρίζεσθαι πρὸς ἀμφότερα,
μήτε τοῖς δεδιττομένοις μήτε τοῖς κολακεύουσιν
ἐνδιδόντας.

ὁ μὲν οὖν Θουκυδίδης, ὡς ἀναγκαίως ἑπομένου
τῷ δύνασθαι τοῦ φθονεῖσθαι,

"καλῶς (φησι) βουλεύεσθαι τὸν ἐπὶ μεγίστοις
λαμβάνοντα τὸ ἐπίφθονον"·

ἡμεῖς δὲ τὸν μὲν φθόνον διαφεύγειν οὐ [οὐ (not) is
omitted by De Lacy and Einarson] χαλεπὸν ἡγού-
μενοι, τὸ δὲ μέμψει μὴ περιπεσεῖν μηδὲ λυπηρόν
τινι γενέσθαι τῶν χρωμένων ἀδύνατον παντάπασιν
ὁρῶντες ὀρθῶς βουλευσόμεθα τὰς τῶν ἀγνωμόνων
ἀπεχθείας ἐκδεχόμενοι μᾶλλον ἢ τὰς τῶν δικαίως
ἐγκαλούντων ἐὰν ἐκείνοις μὴ δικαίως ὑπουργῶμεν.

Most people do realize it, though, and they're fully aware that they're making a mistake. They're like people forced to down a huge glass of wine: they do as they're told, but barely, and with a groan, and scrunching up their face.[31]

9. Welcome Criticism from Bullies

[18] Such cowardice of mind resembles a body that's equally susceptible to heat and cold. You see, such people simply become putty when praised by bullies, but they cringe and panic at criticism and dirty looks if they tell a bully no. We need to stay tough against *both*, giving in to neither intimidation nor flattery.

Thucydides does say, in stating that hatred inevitably follows power [2.64.5, Pericles speaking],

> "He who incurs hatred for the hardest decisions
>   makes good decisions."

And true, you and I don't consider it difficult to avoid *hatred*. Still, it's obviously just plain impossible to *not* offend or get criticized by some of the people we interact with in life. We'll be making the right decision, therefore, to welcome hostility from unreasonable people rather than hostility from those who would, if we "helped" those unreasonable people inappropriately, quite appropriately call us out on it.

καὶ μὴν ἔπαινόν γε τὸν παρὰ τῶν δυσωπούντων κίβδηλον ὄντα παντάπασι δεῖ φυλάττεσθαι καὶ μὴ πάθος πάσχειν ὑῶδες, ὑπὸ κνησμοῦ καὶ γαργαλισμοῦ παρέχοντα χρῆσθαι ῥᾷστα τῷ δεομένῳ, καὶ καταβάλλειν ἑαυτὸν ὑποκατακλινόμενον. οὐδὲν γὰρ διαφέρουσι τῶν τὰ σκέλη τοῖς ὑποσπῶσι παρεχόντων οἱ τὰ ὦτα τοῖς κολακεύουσι παραδιδόντες, ἀλλ᾽ αἴσχιον ἀνατρέπονται καὶ πίπτουσιν, οἱ μὲν ἔχθρας καὶ κολάσεις ἀνιέντες ἀνθρώποις πονηροῖς ἵν᾽ ἐλεήμονες καὶ φιλάνθρωποι καὶ συμπαθεῖς κληθῶσιν, οἱ δὲ τοὐναντίον ἀπεχθείας καὶ κατηγορίας οὐκ ἀναγκαίας οὐδὲ ἀκινδύνους ἀναδέξασθαι πεισθέντες ὑπὸ τῶν ἐπαινούντων ὡς μόνους ἄνδρας καὶ μόνους ἀκολακεύτους καὶ νὴ Δία στόματα καὶ φωνὰς προσαγορευόντων. διὸ καὶ Βίων ἀπείκαζε τοὺς τοιούτους ἀμφορεῦσιν ἀπὸ τῶν ὤτων ῥᾳδίως μεταφερομένοις. ὥσπερ

– Ἀλεξῖνον ἱστοροῦσι τὸν σοφιστὴν πολλὰ φαῦλα λέγειν ἐν τῷ περιπάτῳ περὶ Στίλπωνος τοῦ Μεγαρέως, εἰπόντος δέ τινος τῶν παρόντων, "ἀλλὰ μὴν ἐκεῖνός σε πρώην ἐπῄνει," "νὴ Δία (φάναι)· βέλτιστος γὰρ ἀνδρῶν ἐστι καὶ γενναιότατος."
– ἀλλὰ Μενέδημος τοὐναντίον, ἀκούσας ὡς Ἀλεξῖνος αὐτὸν ἐπαινεῖ πολλάκις,

Furthermore, since praise from bullies is surely phony, we simply *must* be on guard against it. We must not do the pig thing, where we enjoy being scratched and tickled so much that we allow our petitioner to handle us as he likes and we flop down in submission. You see, the only difference between giving ear to a flatterer and leaving our legs exposed to a wrestler is that the throw and fall are more shameful. Hence, some go easy on wrongdoers, so they'll be called "merciful" and "understanding" and "compassionate." Others get seduced by praise into picking unnecessary fights or risky legal battles: they're "the only *real* man" and "the only one of us beyond flattery" and even, by Zeus almighty, "our mouthpiece" and "our voice." (That's why Bion said such people are amphoras: they're easily "carried away" by their "ears."[32]) We're told, for example, that

- In a lecture hall, the sophist Alexinus was saying a lot of nasty things about Stilpon of Megara. When a bystander protested, "But he was saying nice things about *you* the other day," Alexinus replied,

    "Quite right! He's a very fine, top-quality gentleman."
- Menedemus, by contrast, heard that Alexinus was always saying nice things about *him*, and quipped,

"ἐγὼ δέ (εἶπεν) ἀεὶ ψέγω Ἀλεξῖνον· ὥστε
κακός ἐστιν ἄνθρωπος ἢ κακὸν ἐπαινῶν ἢ
ὑπὸ χρηστοῦ ψεγόμενος."

οὕτως ἄτρεπτος ἦν καὶ ἀνάλωτος ὑπὸ τῶν τοιούτων
καὶ κρατῶν ἐκείνης τῆς παραινέσεως ἣν ὁ Ἀντισθέ-
νειος Ἡρακλῆς παρήνει τοῖς παισί, διακελευόμενος
μηδενὶ χάριν ἔχειν ἐπαινοῦντι· τοῦτο δὲ ἦν οὐδὲν
ἄλλο ἢ μὴ δυσωπεῖσθαι μηδὲ ἀντικολακεύειν τοὺς
ἐπαινοῦντας.
    ἀρκεῖ γὰρ οἶμαι τὸ τοῦ Πινδάρου πρὸς τὸν λέγοντα
πανταχοῦ καὶ πρὸς πάντας ἐπαινεῖν αὐτὸν εἰπόντος,

    "κἀγώ σοι χάριν ἀποδίδωμι· ποιῶ γάρ σε ἀληθεύειν."

[19] Ὁ τοίνυν πρὸς πάντα τὰ πάθη χρήσιμόν ἐστι,
τούτου δεῖ μάλιστα τοῖς εὐδυσωπήτοις· ὅταν ἐκβια-
σθέντες ὑπὸ τοῦ πάθους παρὰ γνώμην ἁμάρτωσι καὶ
διατραπῶσιν, ἰσχυρῶς μνημονεύειν καὶ τὰ σημεῖα τοῦ
δηγμοῦ καὶ τῆς μεταμελείας θεμένους ἐν ἑαυτοῖς ἀνα-
λαμβάνειν καὶ φυλάττειν ἐπὶ πλεῖστον χρόνον.

"I've never done anything but criticize
Alexinus, so that must mean he's a bad
man: he either *likes* a bad man, or he's
disliked by a *good* man."

That's how unmoving and impregnable Menedemus
was against such types. He'd mastered the advice
Antisthenes has Hercules give his sons: "Be grateful
to no one for their praise."[33] This was simply another way of saying not to feel pressured by those
who praise us and not to flatter them in return.

On that note, I think a remark of Pindar's suf-
fices. When a man told Pindar that he praised him
always and to everyone, he replied:

"And I thank you in turn, for I will ensure you're
telling the truth."[34]

10. Memory Is the Best Antidote to Caving Again

[19] Now, the same technique that works for all
emotions works especially well for pushovers.
Namely, when dysopia compels people to go against
their better judgment and they get overwhelmed,
they should *remember* the feeling—*really* remember it. They should make mental notes of the remorse and regret, and keep and revisit them for a
very long time.

ὡς γὰρ οἱ λίθῳ προσπταίσαντες ὁδοιπόροι ἢ περὶ
ἄκραν ἀνατραπέντες κυβερνῆται, ἂν μνημονεύωσιν,
οὐκ ἐκεῖνα μόνον ἀλλὰ καὶ τὰ προσόμοια φρίττοντες
καὶ φυλαττόμενοι διατελοῦσιν, οὕτως οἱ τὰ τῆς δυσωπίας αἰσχρὰ καὶ βλαβερὰ συνεχῶς τῷ μετανοοῦντι
καὶ δακνομένῳ προβάλλοντες ἀντιλήψονται πάλιν
ἑαυτῶν ἐν τοῖς ὁμοίοις καὶ οὐ προήσονται ῥᾳδίως
ὑποφερομένους.

— ΤΕΛΟΣ —

You see, if out-of-towners remember when they trip on a cobblestone or sailors remember when they wreck off a headland, they become wary going forward. They protect themselves not only against those specific hazards, but similar ones, too. In the same way, you should dwell on the shame and harm that caving causes, and on the remorse and regret. If you do, you'll resist it in your own similar cases, and you won't let yourself knuckle under so easy again.

— THE END —

A CODA ON SURVIVING A SIEGE

When you push back against an inappropriate request today, it's common to hear the rejoinder "Hey, man, I'm just asking questions." Your petitioner resorts to this line under the false pretense or belief that his or her request is neutral—because, come on, aren't you free to say no? And aren't we all equals anyway?

Everyone understands that this is untrue. Some requests are inherently *unequal, just as some requests are inherently exploitative, predatory, or immoral. The pressure is there by design. In such times you may feel like you're under siege. If so—and before it happens again—you would do well to ponder some wise words from the ancient military tactician known to us as Aeneas Tacticus. They appear at the start of his fourth-century BCE manual* How to Survive Under Siege:

Ὅσοις τῶν ἀνθρώπων ἐκ τῆς αὐτῶν ὁρμωμένοις χώρας ὑπερόριοί τε ἀγῶνες καὶ κίνδυνοι συμβαίνουσιν, ἄν τι σφάλμα γένηται κατὰ γῆν ἢ κατὰ θάλασσαν, ὑπολείπεται τοῖς περιγιγνομένοις αὐτῶν οἰκεία τε χώρα καὶ πόλις καὶ πατρίς, ὥστε οὐκ ἂν ἄρδην πάντες ἀναιρεθείησαν· τοῖς δὲ ὑπὲρ τῶν μεγίστων μέλλουσι κινδυνεύειν, ἱερῶν καὶ πατρίδος καὶ γονέων καὶ τέκνων καὶ τῶν ἄλλων, οὐκ ἴσος οὐδὲ ὅμοιος ἀγών ἐστιν, ἀλλὰ σωθεῖσι μὲν καὶ καλῶς ἀμυναμένοις τοὺς πολεμίους φοβεροὺς τοῖς ἐναντίοις καὶ δυσεπιθέτους εἰς τὸν λοιπὸν χρόνον εἶναι, κακῶς δὲ προσενεχθεῖσι πρὸς τοὺς κινδύνους οὐδεμία ἐλπὶς σωτηρίας ὑπάρξει. τοὺς οὖν ὑπὲρ τοσούτων καὶ τοιούτων μέλλοντας ἀγωνίζεσθαι οὐδεμιᾶς παρασκευῆς καὶ προθυμίας ἐλλιπεῖς εἶναι δεῖ, ἀλλὰ πολλῶν καὶ παντοίων ἔργων πρόνοιαν ἑκτέον, ὅπως διά γε αὐτοὺς μηδὲν φανῶσι σφαλέντες.

A CODA ON SURVIVING A SIEGE

When people set out from their country to face strife and peril in foreign lands and meet with some disaster by land or sea, the survivors still have their own soil and city and homeland to go back to, so all is not lost. But for those who are about to risk everything to defend what is most important to them—their temples, their homeland, their parents and children and all the rest—the struggle is not the same or even similar. You see, if they put up a fierce resistance and save themselves, they will intimidate their enemies and seem invincible forever after; but if they fail to impress in the face of danger, they will have no hope of salvation. Therefore, those who are to fight for such high stakes must not fall short in any preparation or effort. They must keep planning out all kinds of actions, so that should they fail, at least it won't seem to be because of them.

Psychomachia

AURELII CLEMENTIS PRUDENTII

SLAYING YOUR DEMONS

Armageddon in Mind

PRUDENTIUS

A Model of Recovery

*Prudentius prefaces his poem with a magnificent
parable of addiction and recovery compiled from
episodes in the Book of Genesis. Although he explains its meaning in lines 50–68, it will make more
sense after one reads the main poem. The point to
note here is that Lot symbolizes the addict, Abraham the faith and determination that can save him,
the posse of serfs our willpower and efforts, Sarah's
pregnancy the redemption of Lot's—and our—soul,
and their late-born child, the inner peace that comes
of wisdom at long last . . . because it's never too late
to wise up and turn our lives around.*

Senex fidelis prima credendi via
Abram, beati seminis serus pater,
adiecta cuius nomen auxit syllaba,
Abram parenti dictus Abraham deo,
senile pignus qui dicavit victimae   5
docens ad aram cum litare quis velit
quod dulce cordi quod pium quod unicum
deo libenter offerendum credito,
pugnare nos et [Fontaine: *nosmet* vulgate] cum
    profanis gentibus
suasit suumque suasor exemplum dedit   10
nec ante prolem coniugalem gignere
deo placentem, matre virtute editam,
quam strage multa bellicosus spiritus
portenta cordis servientis vicerit.

Victum feroces forte reges ceperant   15
Loth inmorantem criminosis urbibus
Sodomae et Gomorrae, quas fovebat advena
pollens honore patruelis gloriae.
Abram sinistris excitatus nuntiis
audit propinquum sorte captum bellica   20
servire duris barbarorum vinculis.
Armat trecentos terque senos vernulas,
pergant ut hostis terga euntis caedere,
quem gaza dives ac triumfus nobilis
captis tenebant inpeditum copiis.   25

An ancient man of faith was the archetype
of belief. His seed was blessed; at last a father,
Abram—whose name a syllable enlarged
(he was "Abram" to his father, "Abraham" to God)
—offered up that late-born son . . . for sacrifice!   5
He taught us at that altar if we want
to please God, we must trust Him and renounce
our nearest, dearest love, our one and all.
  He inspired us, too, to *fight!* unholy hordes

(and our inspirer demonstrated how   10
himself), and have no children of our own,
which—born of Mother Virtue—would please God,
until our psyche goes to war and slays
the demons, one and all, that rule our heart.

  A captive! Vicious kings took Lot in war.   15
He'd hung around too long in dens of sin:
Sodom and Gomorrah. Though an outsider,
he loved them, and was popular, thanks to his uncle.
  The dire news spurs Abram into action.
"Your nephew's taken captive in the war!   20
He's now enslaved to hard barbarian chains."
He calls and arms three hundred eighteen serfs.
They tail the enemy—and mow them down.
Rich treasures and their prisoner parade
had bogged them down while marching, to their
    doom.   25

Quin ipse ferrum stringit et plenus deo
reges superbos mole praedarum graves
pellit fugatos, sauciatos proterit;

frangit catenas et rapinam liberat:
aurum puellas parvulos monilia   30
greges equarum vasa vestem buculas.
Loth ipse ruptis expeditus nexibus
adtrita bacis colla liber erigit.
Abram triumfi dissipator hostici
redit recepta prole fratris inclytus   35
ne quam fidelis sanguinis prosapiam
vis pessimorum possideret principum.

Adhuc recentem caede de tanta virum
donat sacerdos ferculis caelestibus,
dei sacerdos rex et idem praepotens   40
origo cuius fonte inenarrabili
secreta nullum prodit auctorem sui
Melchisedec, qua stirpe quîs maioribus
ignotus uni cognitus tantum deo.

Mox et triformis angelorum trinitas   45
senis revisit hospitis mapalia,
et iam vietam Sarra in alvum fertilis
munus iuventae mater exsanguis stupet
herede gaudens et cachinni paenitens.

And as for those smug, plunder-bloated kings,
Abram unsheathes his sword, and filled with God,
repels them—routs them—*tramples!* on their
  wounded.
He breaks the chains and liberates the loot:
gold, and women and children and necklaces   30
and teams of horses and tools and clothes and cattle.
Lot, too, is released, his shackles broken off.
He lifts his ring-chafed neck upright. He's free.
  And Abram, scourge of enemy jubilation,
heads home in glory: *"nephew-rescuer!"*   35
He'll have no scion of the blood of faith
fall prey to rages from outrageous kings . . . !

  Our hero, fresh from slaughtering those men,
is given food from heaven by a priest—
a priest of God, and mighty king to boot,   40
his cryptic origins beyond our ken.
They cannot pinpoint any prior parent.
Melchizedek's his name. His line, his ancestors
are all unknown—except, that is, to God. . . . [35]

  A trinity of angels in three guises   45
is welcomed into agèd Abram's hut.
And Sarah, drained of motherhood, cannot
believe! the gift—a child—in her old womb.
Delighted with an heir, she rues her laughter. . . .

Haec ad figuram praenotata est linea   50
quam nostra recto vita resculpat pede:
vigilandum in armis pectorum fidelium
omnemque nostri portionem corporis
quae capta foedae serviat libidini
domi coactis liberandam viribus,   55
nos esse large vernularum divites,
si quid trecenti bis novenis additis
possint figura noverimus mystica.
Mox ipse Christus, qui sacerdos verus est,
parente natus alto et ineffabili   60
cibum beatis offerens victoribus
parvam pudici cordis intrabit casam
monstrans honorem trinitatis hospitae.
Animam deinde spiritus conplexibus
pie maritam, prolis expertem diu,   65
faciet perenni fertilem de semine,
tunc sera dotem possidens puerpera
herede digno patris inplebit domum.

These episodes foretell and made a model   50
our lives should craft anew, on surer foot.
Let's be alert—in arms—with hearts of faith,
and liberate our every body part
that's captive and enslaved to foul desire—
through forces we can call to arms at home.   55
We're lavishly supplied with inborn serfs
—provided that we grasp the mystic sum
Three hundred and eIgHteen in all its power.[36]
Then Christ Himself, the *true* priest, and the Son
begotten of a Father beyond all telling   60
will bring His blissful champions a meal.
He'll come into their humble heart's abode,
in thanks for welcoming the trinity.
And *then* the Holy Spirit will embrace
the lonely soul, and, with eternal seed,   65
will duly have it wed, to bear a child.
Endowed at last, that soul will bring forth life:
a worthy heir to fill the Father's home.

■ ■ ■

HOW TO HAVE WILLPOWER

Christe, graves hominum semper miserate labores,
qui patria virtute cluis propriaque sed una
(unum namque deum colimus de nomine utroque,
non tamen et solum, quia tu deus ex patre, Christe),
dissere, rex noster, quo milite pellere culpas   5
mens armata queat nostri de pectoris antro,
exoritur quotiens turbatis sensibus intus
seditio atque animam morborum rixa fatigat,
quod tunc praesidium pro libertate tuenda
quaeve acies furiis inter praecordia mixtis   10

obsistat meliore manu. Nec enim, bone ductor,
magnarum virtutum inopes nervisque carentes
Christicolas vitiis populantibus exposuisti.
Ipse salutiferas obsesso in corpore turmas
depugnare iubes, ipse excellentibus armas   15
artibus ingenium quibus ad ludibria cordis
obpugnanda potens tibi dimicet et tibi vincat.

Vincendi praesens ratio est, si comminus ipsas
virtutum facies et conluctantia contra

Invocation of Christ, the Muse

Christ, You have always shown pity for human-kind's burdens of suffering. Glory is Yours for the power and virtue You share with the Father!

(The God that we worship is *one*, you see, al-though we use both names rather than only one, because Christ, You are God from the Father.)

Teach us, our king, what fighting forces our minds are equipped with, and how to eradicate evil within our heart's dark recesses. Sometimes, our feelings unsettle and churn so far that rebellion breaks out within us, and struggling mental illness exhausts us. When they do, what defenses then can best safeguard our freedom? Tell us what line of attack can repel all the demons infesting our souls and defeat them.

You see, good commander-in-chief, You didn't leave us helpless — just weaklings unable to cope. You gave Christians great powers: "virtues" to stave off the onslaught of our worst instincts, the vices. When we're obsessed — our flesh besieged — You're within us, directing squadrons of saving graces Yourself. You *Yourself* are equipping us with excellent mental habits to power our spirits for the fray — to grapple for You, and for You, to conquer.

So, the pathway to victory is clear. We must study the Virtues' aspects — their contours — carefully; and viribus infestis liceat portenta notare.   20

Prima petit campum dubia sub sorte duelli
pugnatura Fides agresti turbida cultu
nuda umeros intonsa comas exerta lacertos.
Namque repentinus laudis calor ad nova fervens
proelia nec telis meminit nec tegmine cingi;   25
pectore sed fidens valido membrisque retectis
provocat insani frangenda pericula belli.

Ecce lacessentem conlatis viribus audet
prima ferire Fidem Veterum Cultura Deorum.
Illa hostile caput falerataque tempora vittis   30
altior insurgens labefactat et ora cruore
de pecudum satiata solo adplicat et pede calcat
elisos in morte oculos; animamque malignam

conversely, the monsters menacing them—and us—all around with their hostile aggression.[37]

The Battle Commences

Level One: Faith vs. Worship of the Old Gods

First stepping onto the field to pair up in a perilous showdown, Faith comes. She's itching to fight, looking wild, disheveled, chaotic—shoulders bare, her hair all a mess, and she's showing her biceps. Newfound ambition is surging, you see, and it's flush for a challenge.

There was no sparing a thought for strapping on weapons or armor! No, she puts faith in a muscular heart and her body unaided. "*Bring* on the dangers of this mad war!" she announces. "I'll break 'em."

No sooner said, an opponent accepts, gathers strength, and approaches. The first who dares take a swing at Faith is . . . Worship of the Old Gods.

Faith takes note of the menacing face, the fine headdress of ribbons. Then, cocking back, she *bashes* away—till her enemy's reeling!

Forcing the bloodstained mouth—it was glutted with animals' lifeblood[38]—into the dirt, Faith stomps. She grinds her heel on the eyes—they're bulging out in death, since the life-breath, foul and

fracta intercepti commercia gutturis artant
difficilemque obitum suspiria longa fatigant.   35
Exultat victrix legio, quam mille coactam
martyribus regina Fides animarat in hostem.
Nunc fortes socios parta pro laude coronat
floribus ardentique iubet vestirier ostro.

Exim gramineo in campo concurrere prompta   40
virgo Pudicitia speciosis fulget in armis,
quam patrias succincta faces Sodomita Libido
adgreditur piceamque ardenti sulpure pinum
ingerit in faciem pudibundaque lumina flammis
adpetit et taetro temptat subfundere fumo.   45

Sed dextram furiae flagrantis et ignea dirae
tela lupae saxo ferit inperterrita virgo
excussasque sacro taedas depellit ab ore.
Tunc exarmatae iugulum meretricis adacto
transfigit gladio. Calidos vomit illa vapores   50
sanguine concretos caenoso, spiritus inde

malignant, is getting choked off. The throat's been crushed, its supply lines are broken. Long-drawn labored gasps are impeding her difficult dying.

Rapturous cheers of victory rise from the legion: a thousand martyrs Queen Faith had enlisted and given new life for the battle. Now she crowns her courageous comrades with flowers for winning glory, and has them put on vestments of shimmering purple.

Level Two: Chastity vs. Lust

Next coming onto the grassy field and determined to duke it out is a virgin named Chastity, gleaming in glorious armor. Lust, whose weapons are torches she has brought from her home city, Sodom, leaps at her, thrusting a sulfurous pitch-coated firebrand directly into her face. She goes straight for those *innocent!* eyes with her blazing flame, since she's trying to fill them with acrid and sickening smoke.

The virgin's undaunted. She scoops up a rock and she smashes the hand and fiery shaft of this ravenous Fury, this hot-blooded vixen! Swatting the torch from her sacrosanct face, she makes the foe drop it. Then, with a thrust of her sword driven deep, she impales the defenseless prostitute's throat.

Lust gags, and she spews out warm exhalations: discharge, thickened by feculent clots of blood.

sordidus exhalans vicinas polluit auras.
"Hoc habet" exclamat victrix regina. "Supremus
hic tibi finis erit, semper prostrata iacebis.
Nec iam mortiferas audebis spargere flammas   55
in famulos famulasve dei, quibus intima casti
vena animi sola fervet de lampade Christi.

¡¿Tene, o vexatrix hominum, potuisse resumptis
viribus extincti capitis recalescere flatu,
Assyrium postquam thalamum cervix Olofernis   60
caesa cupidineo madefactum sanguine lavit
gemmantemque torum moechi ducis aspera Iudith
sprevit et incestos conpescuit ense furores,
famosum mulier referens ex hoste tropaeum
non trepidante manu, vindex mea caelitus audax! 65
¡¿At fortasse parum fortis matrona sub umbra
legis adhuc pugnans, dum tempora nostra figurat,
vera quibus virtus terrena in corpora fluxit,
grande per infirmos caput excisura ministros?

Her disgusting breath is polluting the air all around them. It reeks, and it's poison. "*Got* you!" the conquering queen cries out,

"This is the end of the line for you. So now, lie back—in defeat, and forever.

Never again will you dare interfere in the lives of God's servants, wantonly spreading your heat. Their souls' inner marrow is *chaste*. Their passion is ignited and comes alive and springs into life by *one* light alone: Christ's.

Pfft! Did you actually think—you harasser of humankind!—you could rally and roar back to life with a huff and a puff from a lifeless breath? It went out!—back when Holofernes's neck took a dagger, drenching Assyrian lust in blood, and a room in the horror. Brash Judith scorned, you see, all the jewels in that lecherous leader's bed, and by slashing her sword, discouraged unchaste misbehavior.

Such was the woman who brought back home a notorious trophy. *She* didn't flinch—oh no, not *her*, my avenger from heaven! What did you *think?* That my lady was *weak*!?—because she offered resistance back in the dark-age Old Dispensation? She *prefigured* my era! Now, in these times, true power has entered our temporal bodies. Even a peon can take down a big shot today—can 'behead' him!

¿Numquid et intactae post partum virginis ullum 70
fas tibi iam superest? Post partum virginis, ex quo
corporis humani naturam pristina origo
deseruit carnemque novam vis ardua sevit
atque innupta deum concepit femina Christum,
mortali de matre hominem sed cum patre numen. 75

Inde omnis iam diva caro est, quae concipit illum
naturamque dei consortis foedere sumit.
Verbum quippe caro factum non destitit esse
quod fuerat verbum, dum carnis glutinat usum,
maiestate quidem non degenerante per usum 80
carnis sed miseros ad nobiliora trahente.
Ille manet quod semper erat, quod non erat esse
incipiens; nos quod fuimus iam non sumus, aucti
nascendo in melius. Mihi contulit et sibi mansit.
Nec deus ex nostris minuit sua, sed sua nostris 85
dum tribuit nosmet dona ad caelestia vexit.

Dona haec sunt quod victa iaces, lutulenta Libido,
nec mea post Mariam potis es perfringere iura.
Tu princeps ad mortis iter, tu ianua leti;

Isn't it pointless for you to protest, Lust, now that an untouched virgin has born a child? In that moment—a *birth*, from a *virgin!*—our original bloodline abandoned the nature of human bodies.[39] Since then, a heavenly power on high has sown the flesh new; and, what's more, a woman unwedded conceived a *god*—Christ—who is man in the flesh by His mortal mother, but God with His Father.

All flesh, from that point onward, is godlike— all flesh which receives Him. It takes on the nature of God, for He's made it His partner by treaty. Don't you get it? The Word-made-flesh simply doesn't stop being what it had been—the Word— just because it agglutinates flesh, no! Highness doesn't degenerate because of its human en- fleshment. Rather, it draws and impels wretched humans to reach for the nobler. [*God* stays the same as He always was; what he wasn't, He starts to be; whereas *we* no longer are what we were; we've been raised up, born into better. He's given to me; for Himself, He's abided.[40]] *God*'s nature isn't diminished by *ours*, but rather, in sharing part of His being with us, He has brought us to gifts of the heavens.

Here are those gifts: that you lie in defeat there, dirty Libido, and that you cannot infringe on my liberties, ever since Mary. You are the Royal Road to death, you're the gateway to ruin. By staining

corpora conmaculans animas in Tartara mergis.   90
¡Abde caput tristi iam frigida pestis abysso;
¡occide, prostibulum, manes ¡pete, ¡claudere Averno,
inque tenebrosum noctis ¡detrudere fundum!
Te volvant subter vada flammea, te vada nigra
sulpureusque rotet per stagna sonantia vertex.   95
Nec iam Christicolas, furiarum maxima, temptes,
ut purgata suo serventur corpora regi."

Dixerat haec et laeta Libidinis interfectae
morte Pudicitia gladium Iordanis in undis
abluit infectum, sanies cui rore rubenti   100
haeserat et nitidum macularat vulnere ferrum.
Expiat ergo aciem fluviali docta lavacro
victricem victrix abolens baptismate labem
hostilis iuguli. Nec iam contenta piatum
condere vaginae gladium, ne tecta rubigo   105
occupet ablutum scabrosa sorde nitorem,
catholico in templo divini fontis ad aram
consecrat aeterna splendens ubi luce coruscet.

our bodies with sin, you've been plunging our souls into Hades!

Now you've gone cold, blight. Bury your head in the pit of our sorrows. Die, harlot. Go to hell—to the shades, be locked in a furnace, throw yourself down to the pitch-dark depths, to the realm of the nighttime! There, may rivers of fire roll over you, and may the flood of darkness and brimstone churning toss you in deafening rapids. Never again will you tempt Christ's followers, direst of demons. They, for their king, will keep their bodies pure and respected."

Such were her words, and glad at the death of Lust—she's *killed* her!—Chastity's washing her unclean sword in the waves of the Jordan. Flecks of gore and droplets of pus from the wound she inflicted had spattered and clung to the glittering blade of her sword; it's polluted. Hence, like an expert, she is ritually bathing her edge in the river. It conquered; and she, the conqueror, is cleansing the marks of her foe's throat off with a baptism.

Now that it's purified, she's not content to slide the sword into her sheath for safekeeping; she's worried that rust will taint all its newly washed shimmer with scabrous filth, undetected. So, in a Christian temple, beside its divine fountain altar, she consecrates it, to radiate shimmering light there forever.

Ecce modesta gravi stabat Patientia vultu
per medias inmota acies variosque tumultus   110
vulneraque et rigidis vitalia pervia pilis
spectabat defixa oculos et lenta manebat.
Hanc procul Ira tumens, spumanti fervida rictu,
sanguinea intorquens subfuso lumina felle,
ut belli exsortem teloque et voce lacessit   115
inpatiensque morae conto petit, increpat ore
hirsutas quatiens galeato in vertice cristas.

"En tibi, Martis" ait "spectatrix libera nostri,
excipe mortiferum securo pectore ferrum;
nec doleas quia turpe tibi gemuisse dolorem."   120
Sic ait, et stridens sequitur convicia pinus
per teneros crispata notos et certa sub ipsum
defertur stomachum rectoque inliditur ictu;

Level Three: Patience vs. Anger

Meanwhile, Patience is quietly standing by. She looks grave and not at all moved, even amid the tumultuous battle. Watching intently, she's witnessed the wounding—the organs ripped open, javelins going right through them—and yet she maintains her composure.

Spotting her, Anger is seething—her mouth's bubbling over with foam flecks. Training her bloodshot eyes, which are brimming with venomous bile, Anger baits—with her spear and her voice—this *"pacifist shirker!"*

Then, losing patience, she fires her lance while unleashing a verbal tirade that's shaking the bristling plumes on the top of her helmet:

> "This is for you, you freeloading battleground audience member! This is a shot for that untroubled breast of yours. Take it—it's fatal. Don't let it hurt . . . because crying, you see, well—crying is shameful."

That's what she says, and close on her words of abuse comes the screaming pine shaft hurled through the frolicsome air. It's a bull's-eye; it makes it all the way to her belly: Patience is hit with a kill shot!

sed resilit duro loricae excussa repulsu.
Provida nam virtus conserto adamante trilicem   125
induerat thoraca umeris squamosaque ferri
texta per intortos conmiserat undique nervos.

Inde quieta manet Patientia, fortis ad omnes
telorum nimbos et non penetrabile durans,
nec mota est iaculo monstri sine more furentis   130
opperiens propriis perituram viribus Iram.

Scilicet indomitos postquam stomachando lacertos
barbara bellatrix inpenderat et iaculorum
nube supervacuam lassaverat inrita dextram,
cum ventosa levi cecidissent tela volatu   135
iactibus et vacuis hastilia fracta iacerent,
vertitur ad capulum manus inproba et ense corusco
conisa in plagam dextra sublimis ab aure
erigitur mediumque ferit librata cerebrum.

Aerea sed cocto cassis formata metallo   140
tinnitum percussa refert aciemque retundit
dura resultantem, frangit quoque vena rebellis
inlisum chalybem, dum cedere nescia cassos

But . . . the spear falls to the dust! The inflexible corselet has repelled it. The Virtue, you see, thought ahead, and she is wearing a jacket of steel links, three layers thick, on her body. It's woven from iron-mesh fabric scales interlaced, and all of it braided together with leather.

Patience now stands there unruffled while braving a hailstorm of missiles raining down all around. She's impenetrable—she can take it. Nor is she fazed by the spear of the monster who's going berserk with rage: she is waiting for Anger to burn herself out by her own strength.

Naturally—when that barbarian warrior woman has expended all of her muscles in venting her spleen like a brute, and her hand is useless because she's fatigued it by firing a deluge of missiles (pointlessly, since those scattershot blasts fall short in their random flight), and the broken projectiles litter the ground from her tantrum—Anger's destructive hand now feels for the hilt of her sword blade. Heaving the glinting edge high over her ear for the strike, it pauses—and brings down a blow dead on, hitting right on the cranium!

Ah, but a helmet of bronze (its metal was wrought in a smithy) merely rings under the force of the blow and blunts the blade's edge, its hardness enduring the ricochet. Thanks to a crack in the metal, though, the steel shatters on impact. And she—for whom

excipit adsultus ferienti et tuta resistit.
Ira ubi truncati mucronis fragmina vidit   145
et procul in partes ensem crepuisse minutas,
iam capulum retinente manu sine pondere ferri
mentis inops ebur infelix decorisque pudendi
perfida signa abicit monumentaque tristia longe
spernit et ad proprium succenditur effera letum.   150
Missile de multis quae frustra sparserat unum
pulvere de campi perversos sumit in usus.

Rasile figit humi lignum ac se cuspide versa
perfodit et calido pulmonem vulnere transit.
Quam super adsistens Patientia "vicimus"
      inquit   155
"exultans vitium solita virtute sine ullo
sanguinis ac vitae discrimine. Lex habet istud
nostra genus belli furias omnemque malorum
militiam et rabidas tolerando extinguere vires.
Ipsa sibi est hostis vaesania seque furendo   160
interimit moriturque suis Ira ignea telis."

"quitting" means nothing—parries these pointless attacks and safely resists her assaulter.

Anger—seeing the shards of her dagger now splintered and broken, how the blade has burst into bits and pieces all scattered around her, while she's still tightly clutching the hilt of her weaponless weapon—*now* she's enraged! She flings the ivory aside: it is junk, a traitor, a sign of embarrassing pride. She will brook no reminders! Out of control, at a fever pitch, she's become . . . suicidal. Out of the many missiles she's fired in vain, she now picks one up from the dust of the field. She'll pervert it— because she'll invert it.

Ramming the polished shaft in the dirt with the tip pointed upward, Anger falls on her spear. It rips through her lung, and it's searing.

Standing over her, Patience speaks. "We win," she says simply:

> "Once again, *virtue* prevails against vice running rampant in triumph, all without danger to life or of bloodshed. *These* are the tactics this war's mandate requires: to slay demons—to end a whole host of problems, with all of their maddening strength—*we must simply endure them.* Fury's its own worst enemy, self-destructing in fits of rage; and explosive Anger's blasts backfire and destroy her."

Haec effata secat medias inpune cohortes
egregio comitata viro; nam proximus Iob
haeserat invictae dura inter bella magistrae
fronte severus adhuc et multo funere anhelus   165

sed iam clausa truci subridens ulcera vultu
perque cicatricum numerum sudata recensens
milia pugnarum, sua praemia, dedecus hostis.
Illum diva iubet tandem requiescere ab omni
armorum strepitu captis et perdita quaeque   170
multiplicare opibus nec iam peritura referre.

Ipsa globos legionum et concurrentia rumpit
agmina vulniferos gradiens intacta per imbres.
Omnibus una comes virtutibus adsociatur
auxiliumque suum fortis Patientia miscet.   175
Nulla anceps luctamen init virtute sine ista
virtus, et vidua est quam non Patientia firmat.

After these words, Patience pushes her way through the armies unchallenged.

Coming with her is a heroic man. You see, right by her side is . . . Job! He had clung to his unbowed mentor throughout the hard struggles. Up to this moment his face has been grave, short of breath at the dying.

Now, though, he smiles through it all. He reflects on his boils, now healed, and all of the scars he's acquired in thousands of struggles he's powered through. They're his enemies' shame; for *him*, they are badges of honor.

Finally . . . it's finished. The angel tells Job that he can go home now, far from the stress of the front—and should also make good all his losses many times over from spoils, taking prizes that will never depart him.

She herself strides through the crush of legions and clashing battlelines, making her way unhurt through the death-dealing downpour. Patience is bravely teaming up with all the other Virtues (the only to do so), and lending her efforts as needed. *No* Virtue is risking uncertain encounters without this one Virtue, since—if she lacks reinforcement by Patience—she's naught but a widow.

Forte per effusas inflata Superbia turmas
effreni volitabat equo, quem pelle leonis
texerat et validos villis oneraverat armos,   180
quo se fulta iubis iactantius illa ferinis
inferret tumido despectans agmina fastu.
Turritum tortis caput adcumularat in altum
crinibus, exstructos augeret ut addita cirros
congeries celsumque apicem frons ardua ferret.   185
Carbasea ex umeris summo collecta coibat
palla sinu teretem nectens a pectore nodum;
a cervice fluens tenui velamine limbus
concipit infestas textis turgentibus auras.

Nec minus instabili sonipes feritate superbit   190
inpatiens madidis frenarier ora lupatis,
huc illuc frendens obvertit terga negata
libertate fugae pressisque tumescit habenis.
Hoc sese ostentans habitu ventosa virago
inter utramque aciem supereminet et faleratum   195

Level Four: Humble Attitude vs. Pride

Puffed-up Pride, as it happens, is galloping all through the scattered squadrons, high on a spirited horse that she's draped with a lion's skin and whose muscular shoulders she's burdened with decorative mane-braids. She's riding on all these animal's tresses to garner attention while she looks down, with a sneer, on the rank and file she's inspecting.

High on top of her head, she has piled a towering hairdo: pompadour curls, their ringlet construction enhanced by extensions heaped in a mass, for she aims to project a majestic demeanor. A billowing cape that's encircling her shoulders is tied at her bosom into a tapering knot; it is made of gauze linen. Rippling down from her neck is a streamer: a delicate scarf whose texture swells with the air as it catches the oncoming breezes.

No less proud of himself is her steed—indocile, unbroken. *He* won't be taking some slavering bit in his mouth to control him! Stamping back and forth and gnashing his teeth in resentment (freedom to flee is denied him), he's bridling under the pressure.

Flaunting herself in that fashion, the overinflated virago can't be missed as she looms above the two battle formations.

circumflectit equum vultuque et voce minatur
adversum spectans cuneum, quem milite raro
et paupertinis ad bella coegerat armis
Mens Humilis, regina quidem sed egens alieni
auxilii proprio nec sat confisa paratu.   200
Spem sibi collegam coniunxerat, edita cuius
et suspensa ab humo est opulentia divite regno.

Ergo Humilem postquam male sana Superbia
    Mentem
vilibus instructam nullo ostentamine telis
aspicit, in vocem dictis se effundit amaris: 205
"¿Non pudet, o miseri, plebeio milite claros
adtemptare duces ferroque lacessere gentem
insignem titulis, veteres cui bellica virtus
divitias peperit laetos et gramine colles
imperio calcare dedit? ¡Nunc advena nudus   210
nititur antiquos, si fas est, pellere reges!

¡En qui nostra suis in praedam cedere dextris
sceptra volunt! ¡En qui nostras sulcare novales
arvaque capta manu popularier hospite aratro

As she's parading her bangled horse, her tone and expression menace a little detachment she's stalking, a unit composed of just a few soldiers. They're poorly equipped; they were forced to sign up by Humble Attitude (yes, she's a queen, but she needs other people's help, because she lacks confidence in her own native resources. Hope is the comrade in arms she's enlisted, for Hope has her riches high up above this earth; they reside in the kingdom of heaven.).

So, when Pride (her sanity fading) notices Humble Attitude's weapons are bare-bones cheap—not a showpiece among them—bitterly putting her all in her voice, she unleashes a tirade:

"Aren't you *ashamed*, you pathetic fools, to test *glorious* leaders with this ragtag militia? To challenge in battle a tribe that is *known* for its titles?? Whose warrior prowess—whose *virtue* is warfare!—won them riches in olden times, and the power to trample breadbasket hills underfoot as they like?! Oh, *now* we've a naked upstart trying to drive out ancient kings—if only he's able!

Look at these creatures who would have our scepters pass to their *own* hands as spoils)! *Look* at these creatures so eager to furrow our plowlands fallow, exploit our conquered turf with their

contendunt duros et pellere Marte colonos!   215
Nempe, o ridiculum vulgus, natalibus horis
totum hominem et calidos a matre amplectimur
     artus
vimque potestatum per membra recentis alumni
spargimus et rudibus dominamur in ossibus omnes.
¿Quis locus in nostra tunc vobis sede dabatur,   220
congenitis cum regna simul dicionibus aequo
robore crescebant? Nati nam luce sub una
et domus et domini paribus adolevimus annis,
ex quo plasma novum de consaepto paradisi
limite progrediens amplum transfugit in orbem   225
pellitosque habitus sumpsit venerabilis Adam,
nudus adhuc, ni nostra foret praecepta secutus.

¿Quisnam iste ignotis hostis nunc surgit ab oris
inportunus iners infelix degener amens,
qui sibi tam serum ius vindicat, hactenus exul?   230

Nimirum vacuae credentur frivola famae,
quae miseros optare iubet quandoque futuri
Spem fortasse boni, lenta ut solacia mollem
desidiam pigro rerum meditamine palpent.

immigrant plowshares, and force hardy farmers—
by *war!*—from the lands that they've settled!

Pfft! You ridiculous rabble. On leaving the
womb, we *embrace* a person tight in our arms, its
body still warm from its mother. Into the limbs of
this newborn babe we sprinkle our powers' drive,
and take over its growing bones! There are no ex-
ceptions. Where in all this is there room for *you*,
seeing that meanwhile *our* dominions have grown
as one with the growth of our minions? They are
congenital, joined at the hip! We've been sharing
birthdays, maturing, and coming of age—we, the
house and the master—together ever since the new
creature escaped his Edenic confinement, running
away from the zone and stepping out into the *real*
world. *That* is when 'venerable' Adam adopted his
garments of leather; had he not heeded what *we*
recommend, to this *day* he'd be naked![41]

Who is this nemesis risen from backwaters no-
body's heard of—pestering, heavy-handed, un-
wholesome, baseborn, demented—asserting herself
after all this time? Till now, she's been banished!

Oh, I'm sure her vacuous nonsense is going
to gain credence, telling the wretched to cling to
Hope—that 'possibly,' 'some day,' good may come
their way—because vague reassurances flatter meek
acquiescence, excusing the mere *contemplation* of
action.

¿Quid ni illos Spes palpet iners quos pulvere
   in isto   235
tirones Bellona truci non excitat aere
inbellesque animos virtus tepefacta resolvit?
¿Anne Pudicitiae gelidum iecur utile bello est,
an tenerum Pietatis opus sudatur in armis?

¡Quam pudet, o Mavors et Virtus conscia, talem   240
contra stare aciem ferroque lacessere nugas
et cum virgineis dextram conferre choraeis,
Iustitia est ubi semper egens et pauper Honestas
arida Sobrietas albo Ieiunia vultu
sanguine vix tenui Pudor interfusus aperta   245
Simplicitas et ad omne patens sine tegmine vulnus
et prostrata in humum nec libera iudice sese
Mens Humilis, quam degenerem trepidatio prodit!
Faxo ego sub pedibus stipularum more teratur
invalida ista manus; neque enim perfringere
   duris   250
dignamur gladiis algenti et sanguine ferrum
inbuere fragilique viros foedare triumfo."

Talia vociferans rapidum calcaribus urget
cornipedem laxisque volat temeraria frenis

Isn't it clear in this very arena that idle Hope flatters some of her new recruits? Bellona's alarum is not moving *them*—their valor is fading; it *fails* with nonviolent spirits!

—How could Chastity's frigid demeanor be useful in warfare?

—How is Piety's kindhearted work something sweat out in combat?

Oh, for *shame*, o Mars of our fathers, and Valor, my witness! Shameful facing an army like this, picking battles with lightweights, and squaring off with a chorus of virgins mano a mano!

In their group I see Justice, who is always in need; and a pauper, Honesty; there is Temperance, boring and parched; and there's Fasting, ashen-faced; there's Innocence, all but immaculate, blood-less; naked Sincerity, too—she's unguarded and easily wounded. Stretching herself prostrate in the dirt—not free in her own mind—is Humble Attitude. *She's* baseborn; all the trembling betrays her!

I shall have this anemic army ground underfoot like straw in a field! We *don't* condescend to destroy them in sword fights! Staining steel with their cold blood and having my heroes sullied by some meaningless triumph? Out of the question!"

Such are the feelings she's venting while kicking and spurring her horn-hoofed horse to a furious

hostem humilem cupiens inpulsu umbonis
    equini   255
sternere deiectamque supercalcare ruinam.
Sed cadit in foveam praeceps, quam callida forte
Fraus interciso subfoderat aequore furtim

Fraus detestandis vitiorum e pestibus una
fallendi versuta opifex, quae praescia belli   260
planitiem scrobibus violaverat insidiosis
hostili de parte latens, ut fossa ruentes
exciperet cuneos atque agmina mersa voraret,
ac, ne fallacem puteum deprendere posset
cauta acies, virgis adopertas texerat oras   265
et superinposito simularat caespite campum.
At regina humilis, quamvis ignara, manebat
ulteriore loco nec adhuc ad Fraudis opertum
venerat aut foveae calcarat furta malignae.

Hunc eques illa dolum, dum fertur praepete
    cursu,   270
incidit et caecum subito patefecit hiatum.
Prona ruentis equi cervice involvitur ac sub
pectoris inpressu fracta inter crura rotatur.

pace. She's flying with reckless abandon, slack on the reins; she is going to *ram!* and humble this rival, flat on the ground with a blow from the horse, and then *trample!* the victim.

All of a sudden, however, Pride *falls!* — headfirst — in a pit trap. (Cunning Deceit had secretly dug it while mining their front line.)

Ah, Deceit! She's one of the toxic, detestable Vices: crafty, a knack for trickery, and, in foreseeing the war, she had marred the field — and fair play — by preparing an ambush of trenches, hidden from enemy sight. She meant for the ditches to intercept the foe's infantry wedge-attacks, and to swallow their lemmings. Then, to ensure no watchful eye could discover the cheating sink, she had covered its open-air tops with a lattice of branches and camouflaged them as regular ground, laying sod all across them. Meanwhile the humble queen, though little suspecting, had been waiting back farther off. She hadn't yet reached Deceit's covert deception, hadn't set foot on the stolen floor, the malevolent pitfall. . . .

This is the trap into which (by mistake) our rider is falling, suddenly baring the unseen hole with her furious gallop. Pitching out over the horse, she is hugging its neck as it drops . . . but swung underneath to its legs by the press of her chest, she gets flattened.

At virtus placidi moderaminis, ut levitatem
prospicit obtritam monstri sub morte iacentis,   275
intendit gressum mediocriter, os quoque parce
erigit et comi moderatur gaudia vultu.

Cunctanti Spes fida comes succurrit et offert
ultorem gladium laudisque inspirat amorem.
Illa cruentatam correptis crinibus hostem   280
protrahit et faciem laeva revocante supinat.
Tunc caput orantis flexa cervice resectum
eripit ac madido suspendit colla capillo.
Extinctum vitium sancto Spes increpat ore:

"Desine grande loqui, frangit deus omne
        superbum.   285
Magna cadunt, inflata crepant, tumefacta premuntur.
Disce supercilium deponere, disce cavere
ante pedes foveam quisquis sublime minaris.
Pervulgata viget nostri sententia Christi
scandere celsa humiles et ad ima redire feroces. 290

Vidimus horrendum membris animisque Golian
invalida cecidisse manu; puerilis in illum

Meanwhile, the Virtue's in calm control. She sees that the monster's vanity is crushed underfoot and that she is lying near death. Therefore, at a leisurely pace she walks over and lifts her face, slightly. Holding back joy with a courtly expression, she's . . . starting to waver.

Hope, her trusty companion, comes racing to help with an offer: *vengeance!* — a sword — and she's raising her spirits with love of distinction.

Grabbing a hank of hair, Humble Attitude drags out her mangled enemy, bloodied and broken. She pulls and tilts the face upward; then, amid pleas for mercy, she's bending the neck, and she's slicing. Ripping the head off, she lifts it in triumph and dangles the gory scalp by the hair.

Pious Hope now chastens the Vice in extinction:

"End your grandiloquent talk; God breaks down everything prideful: 'greatness' falls, all gassiness fizzles, swelling pops like a pimple. Learn to relax and stop putting on airs. Learn to watch out for pitfalls under your feet — you and *anyone* threatening 'greatness.' Everyone, everywhere, has heard and repeats our messiah's pronouncement: *The humble ascend to the heights, the aggressive go back to the bottom.*[42]

Thus, we witnessed Goliath — a monster in body and spirit — felled by one anemic arm. A little boy's

dextera funali torsit stridore lapillum
traiectamque cavo penetravit vulnere frontem.
Ille minax rigidus iactans truculentus amarus   295
dum tumet indomitum, dum formidabile fervet,
dum sese ostentat, clipeo dum territat auras
expertus pueri quid possint ludicra parvi
subcubuit teneris bellator turbidus annis.

Me tunc ille puer virtutis pube secutus   300
florentes animos sursum in mea regna tetendit,
servatur quia certa mihi domus omnipotentis
sub pedibus domini meque ad sublime vocantem
victores caesa culparum labe capessunt."

Dixit et auratis praestringens aëra pinnis   305
in caelum se virgo rapit. Mirantur euntem
virtutes tolluntque animos in vota volentes
ire simul, ni bella duces terrena retardent.
Confligunt vitiis seque ad sua praemia servant.

hand, see, fired, with a treble *zzzoooww* of his sling, a pebble straight at him, striking and piercing his forehead and causing a deep laceration. So did that menacing, arrogant, bitter, truculent blowhard— swell as he might like an animal, rage as he might like a terror, pound his chest as he might and brandish his shield at the breezes—*so* he found out for *himself* what a little boy's toy can accomplish; *so* was the blustering champion felled by an innocent child!

Then, as his greatness matured, that child decided to follow me. He directed his growing sense of himself to my kingdom, upward. He knew that a house is reserved for me at the feet of our almighty Lord, and that, when I call them to grandeur, it's to *me* that survivors cling when they've slaughtered their demons."

Having concluded her lecture, the maiden takes off for the heavens, skimming the air on golden wings. The Virtues are watching, awed, and lifting their hearts in prayer; they *long* to go with her, truly, and *would*—if the war here below didn't need them to lead it. So they fight on against Vices; they'll wait for their own recognition.

Venerat occiduis mundi de finibus hostis   310
Luxuria extinctae iam dudum prodiga famae,
delibuta comas, oculis vaga, languida voce,
perdita deliciis, vitae cui causa voluptas,
elumbem mollire animum petulanter amoenas
haurire inlecebras et fractos solvere sensus.   315
Ac tunc pervigilem ructabat marcida cenam,
sub lucem quia forte iacens ad fercula raucos
audierat lituos atque inde tepentia linquens
pocula lapsanti per vina et balsama gressu
ebria calcatis ad bellum floribus ibat.   320

Non tamen illa pedes, sed curru invecta venusto
saucia mirantum capiebat corda virorum.

O ¡nova pugnandi species! Non ales harundo
nervum pulsa fugit nec stridula lancea torto
emicat amento frameam nec dextra minatur,   325
sed violas lasciva iacit foliisque rosarum
dimicat et calathos inimica per agmina fundit.

Level Five: Temperance vs. Indulgence

Out of the western ends of the earth comes a new foe, Indulgence, one for whom reputation means nothing (she long ago lost it): perfumed curlicues, restless eyes, with a voice bored and languid. Wrecked by excessive refinement, her reason for living is pleasure: blunting her mind till it's flaccid, abusing and bingeing on soothing drugs and the like to dissolve and escape and to deaden her senses.

This time too she's hungover; she's nauseous from last night's extended party. You see, as she lay there at table and dawn was approaching, trumpet alarums reached her ears. So, dropping her tepid drink, she staggered her way through puddles of wine and perfume and, drunkenly stepping on flowers as she went, headed out to the battle.

(Not as a "foot" soldier, though! She went riding an eye-catching chariot, and, as she rode, she arrested the hearts of admiring contingents.)

Oh, what a strange scene of fighting this is! There's no feathered arrow fleeing its string with a twang, no screaming javelin firing off from a snap of a sling; there are no hands brandishing broadswords. Rather, for bullets she's tossing out violets and blandishing rose petals, teasingly flinging out baskets of flowers among enemy units.

Inde eblanditis virtutibus halitus inlex
inspirat tenerum labefacta per ossa venenum
et male dulcis odor domat ora et pectora et arma 330
ferratosque toros obliso robore mulcet.
Deiciunt animos ceu victi et spicula ponunt
turpiter heu dextris languentibus obstupefacti,
dum currum varia gemmarum luce micantem
mirantur, dum bratteolis crepitantia lora   335
et solido ex auro pretiosi ponderis axem
defixis inhiant obtutibus et radiorum
argento albentem seriem quam summa rotarum
flexura electri pallentis continet orbe.

Et iam cuncta acies in deditionis amorem   340
sponte sua versis transibat perfida signis
Luxuriae servire volens dominaeque fluentis
iura pati et laxa ganearum lege teneri.
Ingemuit tam triste nefas fortissima virtus
Sobrietas dextro socios decedere cornu   345
invictamque manum quondam sine caede perire.

Having enticed the Virtues, the alluring, illicit aroma is breathing delicate venom all through their faltering bones. The sickly sweet bouquet is overcoming mouth, mind, and weapons, gently massaging their ironclad muscles and crushing their mettle. . . .

Losing resolve, like men in defeat, they are dropping their weapons—shamefully, oh!—from languid hands, overawed by the chariot. First, they're amazed how its gemstones radiate all different colors; next, they're agog at the gold-plated reins, which are clicking and clacking; then there's the axle of solid gold, its value enormous; lastly, their longing eyes are obsessed with the series of gleaming spokes, all silvery white and enclosed by rims on the outside curve of the wheels, made of yellow electrum (or maybe it's amber?). . . .

Suddenly, all of the army is transported by dreams of surrender: they—of their own free will—will *defect*, they'll *reverse* their allegiance! Now, they're to be willing *slaves* of Indulgence; they'll *welcome* the wanton mistress's dictatorship, gladly *obey* the lax law of the tavern. . . . [43]

Groaning dismay at this blasphemy (shocking!) is the strongest of Virtues, Temperance, aghast that her comrades-in-arms are deserting the righthand wing, and their unit (unbeaten!) is falling apart without bloodshed.

Vexillum sublime crucis, quod in agmine primo
dux bona praetulerat, defixa cuspide sistit
instauratque levem dictis mordacibus alam
exstimulans animos nunc probris, nunc prece
    mixta.   350

"¿Quis furor insanas agitat caligine mentes?
Quo ruitis? Cui colla datis? ¿Quae vincula tandem
(¡pro pudor!) armigeris amor est perferre lacertis,
¿lilia luteolis interlucentia sertis
et ferrugineo vernantes flore coronas?   355
¿His placet adsuetas bello iam tradere palmas
nexibus, ¿his rigidas nodis innectier ulnas,
¿ut mitra caesariem cohibens aurata virilem
conbibat infusum croceo relegamine nardum,
¿post inscripta oleo frontis signacula, ¿per quae 360
unguentum regale datum est et chrisma perenne?

¿Ut tener incessus vestigia syrmate verrat,
¿sericaque infractis fluitent ut pallia membris,
post inmortalem tunicam quam pollice docto
texuit alma Fides dans inpenetrabile tegmen   365
pectoribus lotis, dederat quibus ipsa renasci,

Ramming a spear in the ground, the good leader now raises a lofty banner: the cross she had carried ahead of the vanguard in battle. *She'll* resurrect these volatile troops with words that will bite them! Mixing pleas in among rebukes, she starts whipping their spirits up:

"What *madness* is churning your minds and clouding your senses? *Where* are you off to? *Who's* this you're bowing to? What are these . . . shackles— oh, for *shame!*—you're dreaming of bearing on hands that bear weapons? *Lilies*!? Peeking through yellow arrangements, all interwoven? *Garlands*, bursting into bloom with mahogany florets!? *These* are the chains you'd like to surrender your battle- accustomed hands to? *These* are the knots you'd enmesh your powerful arms in? All so some gold- bedecked bonnet, complete with its marigold rib- bon closure, can tuck up your (masculine!) hair and bathe in conditioner? *After* you've traced the sign of the cross on your forehead in oil!? A sign that has brought you an unguent of *kings* and anoint- ment unending!?

Want to sashay? Have the train of some gown sweeping over your footsteps? Maybe a silken cloak, to cascade on your vulnerable bodies? Please. Don't you have the *immortal* shirt that nurturing *Faith's* deft fingers wove? It's a bulletproof jacket,

¿inde ad nocturnas epulas, ubi cantharus ingens
despuit effusi spumantia damna Falerni
in mensam cyathis stillantibus, uda ubi multo
fulcra mero veterique toreumata rore rigantur?   370
¿Excidit ergo animis eremi sitis, ¿excidit ille
fons patribus de rupe datus quem mystica virga
elicuit scissi salientem vertice saxi?
¿Angelicusne cibus prima in tentoria vestris
fluxit avis, quem nunc sero felicior aevo   375
vespertinus edit populus de corpore Christi?

¡His vos inbutos dapibus iam crapula turpis
Luxuriae ad madidum rapit inportuna lupanar,
quosque viros non Ira fremens non idola bello
cedere conpulerant saltatrix ebria flexit!   380

State, precor, vestri memores, memores quoque
    Christi.
Quae sit vestra tribus, quae gloria, quis deus et rex
quis dominus meminisse decet. Vos nobile Iudae
germen ad usque dei genetricem qua deus ipse

one she bestows on all the baptized souls she's en-
riched and granted rebirth to.

Then what? Perhaps some all-night party,
where an enormous cantharus spits up Falernian
bubbly—both wasteful, and wasted—onto the
counter as ladles force-feed it?[44] Where you'll see
couches bathing in wine and embroidery damp
from vintage dewdrops? Have you *forgotten* your
thirst in the *desert*!? Forgotten how water *gushed*
from rock as a gift to your fathers? How it was
conjured up by the mystical wand, split stone, and
came tumbling downward!? Hadn't the food of *angels* flowed (indeed, flown!) to their parents' earlier
tents?—the same food that a *better-off*, latter-day
people, though they're living in twilight, consume
from the body of Christ?[45]

Please. Nourished by feasts such as *those*, you'll
be carried away by a shameful bout of *Indulgence*,
and enter her dissolute whorehouse!? Men whom
no roar of *Anger*, men whom no idols could
force to surrender in war, are knuckling under to
some . . . drunken dancer!

Stop this. Remember yourselves and remember,
as well, the Messiah.[46] Think of your tribe—of its
glory—of who your God and your King is, of who
your *Lord* is! Remember these things, for *you* are
the highborn scions of *Judah*!—right down to the
Mother of God, from whom God *Himself* became

esset homo, procerum venistis sanguine longo. 385
Excitet egregias mentes celeberrima David
gloria continuis bellorum exercita curis;

excitet et Samuel, spolium qui divite ab hoste
adtrectare vetat nec victum vivere regem
incircumcisum patitur, ne praeda superstes 390
victorem placidum recidiva in proelia poscat.
Parcere iam capto crimen putat ille tyranno,
at vobis contra vinci et subcumbere votum est.
Paeniteat per si qua movet reverentia summi
numinis hoc tam dulce malum voluisse nefanda 395
proditione sequi; si paenitet, haud nocet error.

Paenituit Ionatham ieiunia sobria dulci
conviolasse favo sceptri mellisque sapore
heu male gustato, regni dum blanda voluptas
oblectat iuvenem iurataque sacra resolvit. 400
Sed quia paenituit nec sors lacrimabilis illa est
nec tinguit patrias sententia saeva secures.
En ego Sobrietas, si conspirare paratis,
pando viam cunctis virtutibus, ut malesuada

man. You descend, therefore, from a long line of princes . . . !

So, let the echoing glory of *David* awaken your noble spirits! He, too, was put to the test by continuous warfare.

Samuel, too. When a wealthy enemy is vanquished, he bans all touching the spoils and letting their king live if he's uncircumcised; and so, no leftover loot or survivor can tempt the victor—who's now at peace—and require a relapse of struggle.[47]

Samuel thinks that it's criminal sparing a tyrant held captive. You, on the other hand, pray for *defeat*, and you yearn to give *in*!

Repent, therefore!—in the name of all reverence (if any) you feel for God almighty—for wanting to follow so sweet of an evil.[48] It's a betrayal of God; but repent, and the error is harmless.

Jonathan also repented for breaking a temperate fast with sweets; he kept licking his lips at the honey—and honey-dipped scepter. Oh, how misguided to *taste* them!—because the seductive delight of *kingship* thrilled the young man, sabotaging his solemn commitment. But—because he *repented*—his fate is no reason to cry: a father's axe did *not* get stained by a merciless sentence![49]

So . . . here I am, I, *Temperance!* And, if you're ready to join me, *I'll* clear the way for *all* of the Virtues! Together we'll make that temptress,

Luxuries multo stipata satellite poenas   405
cum legione sua Christo sub iudice pendat."

Sic effata crucem domini ferventibus offert
obvia quadriiugis lignum venerabile in ipsos
intentans frenos. Quod ut expavere feroces
cornibus obpansis et summa fronte coruscum   410
vertunt praecipitem caeca formidine fusi
per praerupta fugam. Fertur resupina reductis
nequiquam loris auriga comamque madentem
pulvere foedatur, tunc et vertigo rotarum
inplicat excussam dominam; nam prona sub
    axem   415
labitur et lacero tardat sufflamine currum.

Addit Sobrietas vulnus letale iacenti
coniciens silicem rupis de parte molarem,
hunc vexilliferae quoniam fors obtulit ictum
spicula nulla manu sed belli insigne gerenti.   420

Casus agit saxum, medii spiramen ut oris
frangeret et recavo misceret labra palato.
Dentibus introrsum resolutis lingua resectam
dilaniata gulam frustis cum sanguinis inplet.

Indulgence—despite all her cluttering minions—
and her forces, pay a steep price: they'll have the
Messiah to judge them!"[50]

So she avows; and stepping directly in front of the
fiery chariot-horses, she lifts up a crucifix, training
the hallowed wood smack-dab on the reins.

At this, the horses go wild, spooked at the sight
of the outspreading arms and the glint of a "muzzle."[51] Bolting, they burst into panicky, breakneck
flight, running blindly over uneven terrain. Having
hopelessly jerked on the reins, the driver is help-
lessly dragged along on her back, and her glossy
tresses are fouled with dust. Then she's thrown, and
the whirl of the wheels entangles their mistress; she
is wrapped face-first down into the axle. Thus, she
becomes a gruesome brake for the runaway chariot.

As she lies, Temperance comes to deliver the
death blow. She hurls a boulder she finds nearby,
one as huge as a millstone. (Chance had suggested
the standard-bearer resort to ballistics of this kind,
with no spear in hand, just the banner for battle.)

Freefall is driving the stone through the air . . .
till it smashes the breathing holes on her face, and
her lips crush inward and mingle with palate. Teeth
are knocked loose in her mouth, and her tongue has
been shredded to pieces. Chunks of blood are filling
her throat, now torn.

Insolitis dapibus crudescit guttur et ossa   425
conliquefacta vorans revomit quas hauserat offas.

"Ebibe iam proprium post pocula multa cruorem"
virgo ait increpitans. "Sint haec tibi fercula tandem
tristia praeteriti nimiis pro dulcibus aevi.
¡Lascivas vitae inlecebras gustatus amarae   430
mortis et horrificos sapor ultimus asperet haustus!"

Caede ducis dispersa fugit trepidante pavore
nugatrix acies. Iocus et Petulantia primi
cymbala proiciunt; bellum nam talibus armis
ludebant resono meditantes vulnera sistro.   435
Dat tergum fugitivus Amor, lita tela veneno
et lapsum ex umeris arcum faretramque cadentem
pallidus ipse metu sua post vestigia linquit.
Pompa ostentatrix vani splendoris inani
exuitur nudata peplo, discissa trahuntur   440
serta Venustatis collique ac verticis aurum
solvitur et gemmas Discordia dissona turbat.

The unusual feast is making her gag and retch.
She's choking on bone-bits mashed to a pulp and
spitting up globs that she's already swallowed. Temperance gloats:

> "Drink up. After all you've imbibed, you can
> handle your own blood. This regrettable meal is
> final; it's yours, in place of the endless sweets you
> enjoyed in an era that's over. Hedonism must be
> turning to gall as you're tasting the bitter flavor of
> death. May these last swigs take their toll on your
> bingeing!"

Scattering at their general's killing, an army of
clowns goes scurrying off in a tizzy. First, Humor
and Disinhibition throw their cymbals away. You
see, with such weapons they'd played at war, like a
game, as they boxed with shadows and rattled their
noisemakers.

Cupid turns tail like a runaway slave. He aban-
dons his arrows coated with venom, the bow that's
slipped from his shoulders, the falling quiver. Pale
with fear himself, he leaves them behind him. Pomp,
the parader of empty magnificence, drops her pre-
tentious vestments: she's naked. Disarrayed garlands, meanwhile, are trailing out behind Glamor;
gold charms on her neck and the top of her head are
coming apart, and disruptive Disunity's scrambling

Non piget adtritis pedibus per acuta frutecta
ire Voluptatem, quoniam vis maior acerbam
conpellit tolerare fugam; formido pericli   445
praedurat teneras iter ad cruciabile plantas.

Qua se cumque fugax trepidis fert cursibus agmen,
damna iacent: crinalis acus redimicula vittae
fibula flammeolum strofium diadema monile.
His se Sobrietas et totus Sobrietatis   450
abstinet exuviis miles damnataque castis
scandala proculcat pedibus nec fronte severos
conivente oculos praedarum ad gaudia flectit.

Fertur Avaritia gremio praecincta capaci
quidquid Luxus edax pretiosum liquerat unca   455
corripuisse manu pulchra in ludibria vasto
ore inhians aurique legens fragmenta caduci
inter harenarum cumulos. Nec sufficit amplos
inplevisse sinus; iuvat infercire cruminis

their gemstones. Pleasure consents—even though her feet are chafing and raw—to flee through thorny thickets, because a *stronger* compulsion is making her tolerate painful flight: the feeling of *peril!* toughens the soles of her tender feet for the torturous journey.

Everywhere that the escaping procession is fleeing in panic, lost items litter the ground: there's a hairpin, there's ribbons, there's headbands, clasps, a bridal veil, a brassiere, a tiara, a necklace. Temperance herself, and all the soldiers whom Temperance leads, abstain from taking these sloughs as spoils. They curse them and simply trample the tempting traps underfoot. They will not connive at plunder; their austere eyes turn away from the joy of the trappings.

Level Six: Reason (and Action) vs.
Greed (and Deceit)

Greed, so it's said, has gathered her robe to create a deep pocket; and, with the hook of her hand, she's grabbing up anything precious that gluttonous Excess has left behind. Her mouth is wide open, gazing at beautiful trinkets; she's picking out pieces of gold that dropped among piles of sand. Moreover, she isn't content to fill just her roomy pockets; she also likes stashing the filthy

turpe lucrum et gravidos furtis distendere fiscos,   460
quos laeva celante tegit laterisque sinistri
velat opermento. Velox nam dextra rapinas
abradit spoliisque ungues exercet aënos.

Cura Famis Metus Anxietas Periuria Pallor
Corruptela Dolus Commenta Insomnia Sordes, 465
Eumenides variae, monstri comitatus aguntur.
Nec minus interea rabidorum more luporum
crimina persultant toto grassantia campo
matris Avaritiae nigro de lacte creata.

Si fratris galeam fulvis radiare ceraunis   470
germanus vidit conmilito, non timet ensem
exerere atque caput socio mucrone ferire
de consanguineo rapturus vertice gemmas.

Filius extinctum belli sub sorte cadaver
aspexit si forte patris, fulgentia bullis   475
cingula et exuvias gaudet rapuisse cruentas.

lucre in pouches and overstuffed bags that she's cramming with stolen goods. Her left hand is busy concealing the cache, and her left side is crouching over the goods—since her *right* hand is swooping and scraping up plunder and honing its brazen talons on spoils!

Anguish, Hunger, Dread, Anxiety, Perjury, Pallor, Bribery, Hoax, Misrepresentation, Insomnia, Squalor, Haunting Pangs of Remorse are converging: the monster's attendants.

All this time, meanwhile, like ravening wolves, go Atrocities prowling up and down the field and pouncing on victims. Creatures of Greed, they feed on her dark milk—she's their mother:

- When, say, a brother and comrade-in-arms catches sight of his brother's helmet sparkling with yellow-red onyx, he isn't afraid to draw his sword and split the man's skull with a formerly friendly blade—just in order to strip gemstones from the head of a kinsman.
- When, say, after the battle a son's eyes spot the cadaver of his father—killed in war—he happily strips off the harness gleaming with amulet studs, and the blood-stained armor, as spoils.

Cognatam civilis agit Discordia praedam
nec parcit propriis Amor insatiatus habendi
pigneribus spoliatque suos Famis inpia natos.
Talia per populos edebat funera victrix   480
orbis Avaritia sternens centena virorum

milia vulneribus variis. Hunc lumine adempto
effossisque oculis velut in caligine noctis
caecum errare sinit perque offensacula multa
ire nec oppositum baculo temptare periclum.   485

Porro alium capit intuitu fallitque videntem
insigne ostentans aliquid, quod dum petit ille
excipitur telo incautus cordisque sub ipso
saucius occulto ferrum suspirat adactum.

Multos praecipitans in aperta incendia cogit,   490
nec patitur vitare focos quibus aestuat aurum
quod petit arsurus pariter speculator [*peculator*
    "embezzler" some scholars] avarus.

Disunity in the community has them pillaging kins-men, while the insatiable Love of Having prevents them from sparing even their kids, and obscene Hunger, from robbing their children. Such are the faces of death across earth which all the world's conqueror, Greed, produces. She strikes down hundreds of thousands of men with wounds of various kinds. For example,

- A man has lost his sight—his eyes gouged out; she allows him to wander blind, as in nighttime darkness, and stumble his way among obstacles, over and over, absent a cane that could scan for the hazards that lurk all around him.
- Elsewhere, she catches another man's gaze and entraps him with both eyes open. She flashes him something impressive; he goes for it and . . . gets *shanked!* by her sword; he'd never suspected; it cuts to the heart; he lets out a doleful groan of regret that the blade's driven deeply.
- Many she hustles and herds along into obvious fires. She doesn't allow such types to shun flames where there's gold being smelted. Greedy observers reach for that gold—though they're destined to burn, too.

Omne hominum rapit illa genus. Mortalia cuncta
occupat interitu neque est violentius ullum
terrarum vitium, quod tantis cladibus aevum   495
mundani involvat populi damnetque gehennae.
Quin ipsos temptare manu, si credere dignum est,
ausa sacerdotes domini, qui proelia forte
ductores primam ante aciem pro laude gerebant
virtutum, magnoque inplebant classica flatu.   500

Et fors innocuo tinxisset sanguine ferrum,
ni Ratio armipotens, gentis Levitidis una
semper fida comes, clipeum obiectasset et atrae
hostis ab incursu claros texisset alumnos.
Stant tuti Rationis ope, stant turbine ab omni   505
inmunes fortesque animi; vix in cute summa
praestringens paucos tenui de vulnere laedit

cuspis Avaritiae. Stupuit luis inproba castis
heroum iugulis longe sua tela repelli.
Ingemit et dictis ardens furialibus infit: 510

Greed has the whole human race in her clutches; she has infested every affair here below with perdition. There isn't a Vice on earth that's more frightening, because she involves the average person's life in utter disaster and gets him condemned to Gehenna.

Worse, she's even attempting (believe it or not) to go after priests of the Lord themselves! These men have been leading the struggle out at the forefront in battle as needed, upholding the Virtues' merits and fervently filling their trumpets with thunderous huffing.

Greed very well might have dipped her blade in their innocent blood, too . . . had not *Reason!*— master at weapons, the one and forever-faithful aide of the priestly tribe of Levi—held out her shield and protected these glorious wards from the onslaught of darkness. Saved by the actions of Reason, they're standing their ground in the whirlwind, brave and impervious. Greed's sharp projectiles do graze a few, but barely nick their skin; she's leaving them mere superficial wounds at best.

The nefarious plague can't believe what she's seeing: shots she's taking at their pure throats are . . . bouncing away! She lets out a groan and splutters out rage in a furious passion:

"Vincimur heu segnes nec nostra potentia perfert
vim solitam. Languet violentia saeva nocendi,
sueverat invictis quae viribus omnia ubique
rumpere corda hominum; nec enim tam ferrea
      quemquam
formavit natura virum, cuius rigor aera   515
sperneret aut nostro foret inpenetrabilis auro.
Ingenium omne neci dedimus. Tenera aspera dura
docta indocta simul bruta et sapientia nec non
casta incesta meae patuerunt pectora dextrae.
Sola igitur rapui quidquid Styx abdit avaris   520
gurgitibus. Nobis ditissima Tartara debent
quos retinent populos. Quod volvunt saecula
      nostrum est;
quod miscet mundus, vaesana negotia, nostrum.

¿Quî fit praevalidas quod pollens gloria vires
deserit et cassos ludit fortuna lacertos?   525
Sordet Christicolis rutilantis fulva monetae
effigies, sordent argenti emblemata et omnis
thensaurus nigrante oculis vilescit honore.

¿Quid sibi docta volunt fastidia? ¿Nonne triumfum
egimus ex Scarioth, magnus qui discipulorum   530
et conviva dei, dum fallit foedere mensae

"Arrgh! We're losing, *failing!* Our powers aren't having the usual impact they do. Our malevolent force is deteriorating, though in the past its unstoppable strength would demolish the will of *every* human heart. No such constitution of iron ever did shape a man so inflexible that he'll disdain the jingling of brass, or that's wholly beyond any reach of our gold. We've handed death every kind of temperament: sensitive, gruff, hard, cultured as well as uncultured, slow-witted, insightful, and also chaste and perverted—*all* these types have been open to my hand. Hence, *I* alone have dispatched whatsoever the Styx's greedy depths are hoarding; opulent Tartarus owes to *us* all the nations trapped in his realm; the endeavors of whole *generations* belong to *us*, all the *world*'s exertions—such mad striving!—are *ours*, too.

How is this *happening*—glorious *power* deserting triumphant strength? That Fortune is *cheating* our muscles and making them pointless? Golden likenesses stamped on glittering coins are but *filth!* to these Christ worshippers; silver embossings are filth—just as *every* treasure is worthless junk in their eyes, for its merits are darkened.

What does this learned fastidiousness *mean*? Because didn't we conquer Judas Iscariot? *He* was important among the disciples—God's very table companion!—until, at a meal, he betrayed Him

haudquaquam ignarum dextramque parabside iungit?
Incidit in nostrum flammante cupidine telum
infamem mercatus agrum de sanguine amici
numinis, obliso luiturus iugera collo.   535

Viderat et Iericho propria inter funera quantum
posset nostra manus, cum victor concidit Achar.
Caedibus insignis murali et strage superbus
subcubuit capto victis ex hostibus auro,
dum vetitis insigne legens anathema favillis   540
maesta ruinarum spolia insatiabilis haurit.
Non illum generosa tribus, non plebis avitae
iuvit Iuda parens, Christo quandoque propinquo
nobilis et tali felix patriarcha nepote.

Quîs placet exemplum generis, placeat quoque
       forma   545
exitii; sit poena eadem quibus et genus unum est.
¿Quid moror aut Iudae populares aut populares
sacricolae summi (summus nam fertur Aäron)
fallere fraude aliqua Martis congressibus inpar?
Nil refert armis contingat palma dolisve."   550

(though, of course, He knew) when the two joined hands in a bowl. His covetousness engulfed him in flames and flung him on *our* sword—after he'd purchased that evil piece of land from the blood of God, his friend—to atone for those acres by choking his life off.

Jericho, too, in the midst of its own devastation, had witnessed all that our hand can achieve via Achan's downfall in triumph. Noted for numerous killings and proud of their tearing the walls down, Achan succumbed to the gold they'd captured from enemies vanquished. Noting a votive (anathema!) offering among the forbidden ashes, he grabbed it—compulsively bingeing on spoils of destruction.[52] Tribal prestige could do nothing to help him, nor could his fathers' ancestor, Judah, who would one day become famous as kin to Christ, and a patriarch fertile and blessed with so great a descendant.

Those who enjoy his appeal to that lineage should *also* enjoy his death—since identical *punishment* best suits identical *lineage*! Why don't I *trick*, then, Judah's coethnics or the coethnics linked to the highest priest—for they do say that Aaron was "highest"—using *deceit*?[53] I'm *unable* to match them in hand-to-hand fights. It makes no difference whether a win comes by arms or by ruses!"

Dixerat et torvam faciem furialiaque arma
exuit inque habitum sese transformat honestum.
Fit virtus specie vultuque et veste severa
quam memorant Frugi, parce cui vivere cordi est
et servare suum. Tamquam nil raptet avare,   555
artis adumbratae meruit ceu sedula laudem.

Huius se specie mendax Bellona coaptat,
non ut avara luis sed virtus parca putetur;
nec non et tenero Pietatis tegmine crines
obtegit anguinos, ut candida palla latentem   560
dissimulet rabiem, diroque obtenta furori,
quod rapere et clepere est avideque abscondere
    parta,
natorum curam dulci sub nomine iactet.

Talibus inludens male credula corda virorum
fallit imaginibus. Monstrum ferale sequuntur   565
dum credunt virtutis opus. Capit inpia Erinys
consensu faciles manicisque tenacibus artat.
Attonitis ducibus perturbatisque maniplis
nutabat virtutum acies errore biformis
portenti ignorans quid amicum credat in illo   570
quidve hostile notet. Letum versatile et anceps
lubricat incertos dubia sub imagine visus,

Having concluded, she sheds her menacing face and demonic weapons. Greed is reinventing herself as a *good* habit now! She's becoming the Virtue in looks and demeanor and sensible clothing people call Thrift—for whom saving money and living within one's means is important. She's looking as if she would *never* grab something greedily, no! Her detailed imitation is very impressive.

Such is the guise this underhanded Bellona is adopting, angling to pass for a provident Virtue instead of malignant Greed. And what's more, she's even concealing her snake-hair beneath a gossamer veil of "Motherhood," hoping an ivory robe will cloak latent savagery and cover over frenetic psychosis. That way, she'll call all her grabbing and filching and greedily hoarding profits by the delicious name "taking care of the children."

Costumed in such illusions, she's evilly winning the all-too credulous hearts of the men. As they follow the lead of this lethal monster, believing it's Virtue's work, the nefarious demon captures them (they go along gladly) and binds them in shackles.

Meanwhile—its leadership flustered, its infantry in disarray—the Virtue's line is beginning to falter, confused by this two-faced thing. They're unsure as to what to think friendly about her and what to note as hostile. She's lethal, ambiguous, constantly changing shape. Even now, her uncertain appearance is blurring their eyes, when . . .

cum subito in medium frendens Operatio campum
prosilit auxilio sociis pugnamque capessit,
militiae postrema gradu sed sola duello   575
inpositura manum ne quid iam triste supersit.
Omne onus ex umeris reiecerat, omnibus ibat
nudata induviis multo et se fasce levarat,
olim divitiis gravibusque obpressa talentis
libera nunc miserando inopum quos larga benigne 580
foverat effundens patrium bene prodiga censum.
Iam loculos ditata fidem spectabat inanes
aeternam numerans redituro faenore summam.

Horruit invictae Virtutis fulmen et inpos
mentis Avaritia stupefactis sensibus haesit   585
certa mori. Nam ¿quae fraudis via restet, ut ipsa
calcatrix mundi mundanis victa fatiscat
inlecebris spretoque iterum sese inplicet auro?

Invadit trepidam Virtus fortissima duris
ulnarum nodis obliso et gutture frangit   590
exsanguem siccamque gulam; conpressa ligantur

. . . all of a sudden, *Action!* is roaring and leaping right into battle, to succor her allies.[54] She's taking the lead in the fighting, last though she is in the battle formation, for Action alone is going to finish this showdown for good and get rid of the terror.

Flinging every encumbrance off of her shoulders, she's come out stripped of all coverings. She has long since shed most of her burdens. Once, in the past, substantial wealth had weighed heavily on her; now, she's found freedom in helping the poor. She's made ample provision, giving away her family estate—and she gave with abandon. Having grown rich in Faith, she'd examine her empty account books, figuring her net worth for all time—now including the interest.

Thunderstruck by this incredible burst of unconquerable Virtue, Greed is going out of her mind with fear. She's paralyzed, senseless, certain she'll die: Because what manner *now* of deception could get this world's very *disdainer* to crack under pressure to worldly blandishments? Get her to slip back into the gold she'd rejected?

As she's fretting, the bravehearted Virtue *leaps!* at her with a stiff double-forearm strike to the throat. It's crushing, and knocks the wind completely out

vincla lacertorum sub mentum et faucibus artis
extorquent animam, nullo quae vulnere rapta
palpitat atque aditu spiraminis intercepto
inclusam patitur venarum carcere mortem.   595

Illa reluctanti genibusque et calcibus instans
perfodit et costas atque ilia rumpit anhela.
Mox spolia extincto de corpore diripit auri
sordida frusta rudis nec adhuc fornace recoctam
materiam, tiniis etiam marsuppia crebris   600
exesa et virides obducta aerugine nummos

dispergit servata diu victrix et egenis
dissipat ac tenues captivo munere donat.
Tunc circumfusam vultu exultante coronam
respiciens alacris media inter milia clamat: 605

"¡Solvite procinctum, iusti, et discedite ab armis!
Causa mali tanti iacet interfecta. Lucrandi
ingluuie pereunte licet requiescere sanctis.
Summa quies nil velle super quam postulet usus
debitus, ut simplex alimonia, vestis et una   610

of her foe. Action's arms lock a chokehold garrote below Greed's chin, and squeeze. She is wresting the life from Greed's throttled mouth. No external wound is instantly killing Greed—no, she's thrashing in pain all the while that her breathing is being cut, for she's dying a death that's confined to the veins in her body.

Action pins the resisting Vice underfoot with her knees. She *rams!* a knife into her ribs and bursts Greed's heaving intestines.

After the body expires, she strips it of spoils. There's dirty nuggets of unworked gold, other ore that's still unrefined by crucible, even some purses for money that maggots have eaten into, as well as coins gone green from a patina crust.

The champion disperses this long-hoarded stash. To the poor, she distributes items; she's handing out gifts to the broke from the wealth she's recaptured. Then, upon seeing exultant crowds have gathered around, she joyfully lifts up her voice in the midst and among all the thousands:

> "People of justice, unbuckle your gear! Walk away from your weapons! Lying here, slain, is the cause of our troubles. She's done for. Believers now can rest: this suctioning drive to *acquire!* has perished. True serenity lies in no more than necessity calls for—wanting to have just a simple diet, as well

infirmos tegat ac recreet mediocriter artus
expletumque modum naturae non trahat extra.
Ingressurus iter peram ne tollito neve
de tunicae alterius gestamine providus ito
nec te sollicitet res crastina ne cibus alvo   615
defuerit; redeunt escae cum sole diurnae.

¿Nonne vides ut nulla avium cras cogitet ac se
pascendam praestante deo non anxia credat?
Confidunt volucres victum non defore viles,
passeribusque subest modico venalibus asse   620
indubitata fides dominum curare potentem
ne pereant. Tu, cura dei, facies quoque Christi,
¿addubitas ne te tuus umquam deserat auctor?

Ne trepidate, homines; vitae dator et dator
     escae est.
Quaerite luciferum caelesti dogmate pastum   625
qui spem multiplicans alat invitiabilis aevi
corporis inmemores. Memor est qui condidit illud
subpeditare cibos atque indiga membra fovere."

as a basic garment to cover one's infirm limbs, to support and sustain them. Nature's limit, once satisfied, should not be exceeded.

Hence, when you're leaving to go on a journey, don't bring a bag, and go without any regard for an extra shirt to change into. Don't be anxious about circumstances tomorrow, that food will fail your belly. Our daily bread comes again with the sunrise.

Don't you see how none of the birds give a thought to tomorrow? How, without worry, they trust that God will provide for their feeding? Our ubiquitous feathered friends are confident they won't lack for food: even dime-a-dozen sparrows don't doubt the powerful Lord is at pains to ensure their survival—they simply take it on faith. Whereas you—God's love, and Christ's avatar also—are you actually worried your Maker could ever desert you?

People, fear not! Because He who gives life, gives us food in addition. Seek, in our heavenly lore, a repast that brings light and sustains and strengthens our hope in an endless world, one beyond vitiation. Do so, ignoring your body—because the Creator takes care to furnish food to eat. He provides for the needs of His body."

His dictis curae emotae. Metus et Labor et Vis
et Scelus et placitae fidei Fraus infitiatrix   630
depulsae vertere solum. Pax inde fugatis
hostibus alma abigit bellum. Discingitur omnis
terror et avulsis exfibulat ilia zonis.
Vestis ad usque pedes descendens defluit imos
temperat et rapidum privata modestia gressum.   635
Cornicinum curva aera silent; placabilis inplet
vaginam gladius; sedato et pulvere campi

suda redit facies liquidae sine nube diei;
purpuream videas caeli clarescere lucem.
Agmina casta super vultum sensere tonantis   640
adridere hilares pulso certamine turmae
et Christum gaudere suis victoribus arce
aetheris ac patrium famulis aperire profundum.

Dat signum felix Concordia reddere castris
victrices aquilas atque in tentoria cogi.   645
Numquam tanta fuit species nec par decus ulli
militiae, cum dispositis bifida agmina longe

The Triumphant Return

At these words, their anxieties vanish. Fear, Trouble, Violence, Crime, and Deceit—the denier of recognized Faith—quit the country, driven away in defeat.

Thereupon, growth-fostering Peace ousts enemies; she displaces war. All fear is disarmed, the awful equipment thrown aside. They're unfastening buckles; clothing comes streaming down to rest on the top of their ankles. Normal civilian restraint is relaxing their soldierly pacing. Buglers' curves of brass have gone silent; swords are returned to scabbards, appeased, as dust begins settling down in the field.

The brilliant and beautiful face of a cloudless day is returning. Glorious light overhead is beginning to shine—you can see it. Squadrons, relieved that the struggle is over, can sense up above the Thunderer's features smiling down on the ranks of their martyrs and the Messiah's delight at their victory in His ethereal fortress. They sense He's unlocking the Father's unknown for His servants.

Satisfied, Unity signals it's time to return the victorious eagle standards of war to their camp and regather in tents there.

Never has any militia enjoyed a magnificent sight like this, or comparable glory! Detachments are marching in two long column formations. The in-

duceret ordinibus peditum psallente caterva,
ast alia de parte equitum resonantibus hymnis.
Non aliter cecinit respectans victor hiantem   650
Istrahel rabiem ponti post terga minacis,
cum iam progrediens calcaret litora sicco
ulteriora pede stridensque per extima calcis
mons rueret pendentis aquae nigrosque relapso
gurgite Nilicolas fundo deprenderet imo   655
ac refluente sinu iam redderet unda natatum
piscibus et nudas praeceps operiret harenas.

Pulsavit resono modulantia tympana plectro
turba dei celebrans mirum ac memorabile saeclis
omnipotentis opus liquidas inter freta ripas   660
fluctibus incisis et subsistente procella
crescere suspensosque globos potuisse teneri.

Sic expugnata vitiorum gente resultant
mystica dulcimodis virtutum carmina psalmis.
Ventum erat ad fauces portae castrensis,
          ubi artum   665
liminis introitum bifori dant cardine claustra.

fantry troupe is singing out psalms, while opposite them, the cavalry's echoing hymns in responsion.

Much like this was the song the victorious Israel sang while gazing back at the foaming jaws of the furious Sea still looming behind. . . . [55]

> They'd already made it across to the other shore—
> their feet were not even wet—when right on their
> heels, a mountain of water suspended in air crashed
> down; the colliding currents dragged the Nile's black
> denizens down to the seabed. Ebbs recreated a bay
> and provided the fish with a place to swim, while
> the plunging waves covered over the sands they'd
> left naked.
>
> Drumsticks pounding on tambourines to estab-
> lish the rhythm, God's community hymned the
> Almighty's miraculous feat—a feat for the ages: in
> mid-sea, two liquid embankments somehow had
> sliced a path through the waves and grew as the
> wind died down, and they'd somehow managed to
> hold the huge volumes of water.

Such is the Virtues' melodious call-and-response celebrating triumph over the Vices' hordes—a mysterious anthem.

Once they've arrived at the camp gate's jaws, where the double-door hinges block the way in and afford little more than a bottleneck entrance,

Nascitur hic inopina mali lacrimabilis astu
tempestas, placidae turbatrix invida Pacis,
quae tantum subita vexaret clade triumfum.

Inter confertos cuneos Concordia forte,   670
dum stipata pedem iam tutis moenibus infert,
excipit occultum vitii latitantis ab ictu

mucronem laevo in latere. Squalentia quamvis
texta catenato ferri subtegmine corpus
ambirent sutis et acumen vulneris hamis   675
respuerent rigidis nec fila tenacia nodis
inpactum sinerent penetrare in viscera telum,
rara tamen chalybem tenui transmittere puncto
commissura dedit qua sese extrema politae
squama ligat tunicae sinus et sibi conserit oras. 680

Intulit hoc vulnus pugnatrix subdola victae
partis et incautis victoribus insidiata est.

Nam pulsa culparum acie Discordia nostros
intrarat cuneos sociam mentita figuram.

out of the blue they are hit by a storm of deplorable Evil—*tricked!* by rancorous jealousy from a disturber of tranquil Peace: she has come to afflict the great triumph with sudden disaster!

Unity, see, had been caught in a snarl of gridlocked formations funneling in. The moment she's crossing to safety inside, she's *shanked!* in the ribs: it's a dagger, secretly thrust by a lurking Vice, directly at her left side!

Secret Level Seven: Unity vs. Disunity

Although the lamellar weave encasing her body in mail with a webbing of iron links holds stiff; though its interconnected rings of chains have refused the wound's sharp point; though the austere knots' tough threads don't allow the weapon's impact to carry on through and to penetrate vitals— nevertheless, a chink in the plaiting *did* give the steel a tiny point to get in. It's a gap where the otherwise perfect breastplate's outermost scale is fastened and sewn to the hem.

A cunning guerilla, carrying on from the side that's defeated, inflicts this wound. She's been biding her time to surprise the regime.

See, after the Vices' army was routed, Disunity had entered *our* side's formations, disguising herself as an allied combatant! Far back out in the battlefield

Scissa procul palla structum et serpente flagellum   685
multiplici media camporum in strage iacebant.
Ipsa redimitos olea frondente capillos
ostentans festis respondet laeta choraeis;

sed sicam sub veste tegit, te, maxima Virtus,
te solam tanto e numero, Concordia, tristi   690
fraude petens. Sed non vitalia rumpere sacri
corporis est licitum, summo tenus extima tactu
laesa cutis tenuem signavit sanguine rivum.

Exclamat Virtus subito turbata: "¿Quid hoc est?
¿Quae manus hic inimica latet, quae prospera
    nostra   695
vulnerat et ferrum tanta inter gaudia vibrat?
¿Quid iuvat indomitos bello sedasse furores
et sanctum vitiis pereuntibus omne receptum,

si virtus sub pace cadit?" Trepida agmina maestos
convertere oculos. Stillabat vulneris index   700
ferrata de veste cruor. Mox et pavor hostem
comminus adstantem prodit; nam pallor in ore

carnage, close to the center, lie her tattered mantle and lash with its manifold serpents. She herself has been tossing her hair (it's encircled in leafy olive branches), and joyfully singing along with the anthem.

But . . . underneath her clothes, she's been hiding a dagger for *you*, our greatest Virtue. Unity, only you of our many did she attack with her horrible trick—but she wasn't allowed to fatally split your sacred body: only the outer skin that was nicked is now left marked with a trickle of blood.

The Virtue is surprised and confused. She blurts out,

> "What's going on? What enemy hand lies hidden here to disrupt our triumphant joy? Who is unsheathing a *sword* at this time of our great celebration!?
>
> What was the point of reducing the furious demons in battle? Or in retaking the sanctum after the Vices were slain, if Virtue falls in a time of peace?"

The uncomfortable soldiers turn their eyes toward her, distressed, and . . . there's *proof!* she's been wounded: blood—dripping down her chain-mail shirt!

Yet fear soon betrays the enemy standing in their midst, for a face has gone ashen, fully aware of the

conscius audacis facti dat signa reatus
et deprensa tremunt languens manus et color albens.

Circumstat propere strictis mucronibus omnis   705
virtutum legio exquirens fervente tumultu
et genus et nomen, patriam sectamque, deumque
quem colat et missu cuiatis venerit. Illa

exsanguis turbante metu: "Discordia dicor,
cognomento Heresis; deus est mihi discolor"
    inquit,   710
"nunc minor aut maior, modo duplex et modo
    simplex;
cum placet, aërius et de fantasmate visus;
aut innata anima est, quotiens volo ludere numen.
Praeceptor Belia mihi, domus et plaga mundus."

Non tulit ulterius capti blasfemia monstri   715
virtutum regina Fides, sed verba loquentis
inpedit et vocis claudit spiramina pilo
pollutam rigida transfigens cuspide linguam.

rash deed done. It's revealing she's guilty, as do her trembling hand when it's caught, and her whitened complexion.

Whipping out daggers and instantly forming a cordon around her, all of the Virtue legion is demanding, while pushing and shoving,

> "Name! Genealogy! Homeland! Religion! What god do you worship? Tell us at whose behest you've come—and who do they work for?"

Pale and flustered with fear, she replies:

> "Disunity's what they call me; my last name is Heresy, and my god is of a ... *different* hue— maybe weak, maybe great, and at other times double, or single. God, when I so decide, is air and a mere apparition ... or just our inborn soul, when I'm choosing to toy with His godhood. Belial is my teacher; the *world* is my home and my region ... !"[56]

Faith, the queen of the Virtues, will *stand!* for no more of this monstrous prisoner's blasphemies. Moving to censor the speech that she's hearing, Faith shuts down the voice's airway by thrusting a spear; its hardened tip tears through the obscene tongue, and it pins it.

Carpitur innumeris feralis bestia dextris.
frustatim sibi quisque rapit, quod spargat in auras, 720
quod canibus donet, corvis quod edacibus ultro
offerat, inmundis caeno exhalante cloacis
quod trudat, monstris quod mandet habere marinis.
Discissum foedis animalibus omne cadaver
dividitur, ruptis Heresis perit horrida membris. 725

Conpositis igitur rerum morumque secundis
†in commune bonis tranquillae plebis ad unum
sensibus in tuta valli statione locatis,†[57]   728
exstruitur media castrorum sede tribunal   730
editiore loco, tumulus quem vertice acuto
excitat in speculam, subiecta unde omnia late
liber inoffenso circum inspicit aëre visus.
Hunc sincera Fides simul et Concordia sacro
foedere iuratae Christi sub amore sorores   735

conscendunt apicem. Mox et sublime tribunal
par sanctum carumque sibi supereminet aequo
iure potestatis; consistunt aggere summo
conspicuae populosque iubent adstare frequentes.

Countless hands are ripping the murderous beast into pieces. Bit by bit, each is grabbing a hunk to throw in the air, or give to the dogs, or offer to feed to the ravenous crows, or shove deep down a disgusting, excrement-stinking and -steaming sewer, or let the sea creatures have it—to have and to chew on.

All the cadaver is rendered to pieces and shared out among the unclean animals. Thus dies threatening Heresy, shredded.

The Speeches of Unity and Faith

Now—with material boons and behavior securely established, creating conditions for people at peace to generally prosper, plus the Emotions protected and safe in the garrison walls—a stage is erected within their camp in a central position.

It's been set on a good elevation, transforming a sharp-tipped hill to an observation post. From here, unobstructed views look out and down all around onto everything under. Sincere Faith and Unity mount this summit as one—as sisters, sharing a sacred bond with each other on oath, and bound by the love of Christ. They're a duo, a match made in heaven.

And, before long, they've ascended the high-up stage, where they tower above it, equal in stature. They stand there united atop the dais, heroically calling their people to come in great numbers.

Concurrunt alacres castris ex omnibus omnes.   740
Nulla latet pars mentis iners quae corporis ullo
intercepta sinu per conceptacula sese
degeneri languore tegat. Tentoria apertis
cuncta patent velis; reserantur carbasa ne quis
marceat obscuro stertens habitator operto.   745

Auribus intentis expectant contio quidnam
victores post bella vocet Concordia princeps
quam velit atque Fides virtutibus addere legem.
Erumpit prima in vocem Concordia tali

adloquio: "Cumulata quidem iam gloria vobis,   750
o patris, o domini fidissima pignera Christi,
contigit. Extincta est multo certamine saeva
barbaries, sanctae quae circumsaepserat urbis
indigenas ferroque viros flammaque premebat.
Publica sed requies privatis rure foroque   755
constat amicitiis. Scissura domestica turbat
rem populi titubatque foris quod dissidet intus.

Everyone, everywhere, pours from the camp and comes rushing together. None of the mind's components remain unaffected and laggard, hoping to hide their degenerate sloth in a body recess and blame it on blocked-up vessels. All the pavilions are open wide, their flaps pulled back and the canvas retracted, to make sure none of the audience dozes off under cover of darkness.

Eager to listen, the meeting is anxious to know why their leader, Unity, is summoning victors now that the war is complete, and what dispensation Faith has in mind to impose on the Virtues.

Unity breaks the silence first. She gives an assessment such as follows:

> "Already the glory is great beyond question, all you faithful fulfillments of Christ our Lord and our Father, which has accrued to you. Your hard-fought battle destroyed those ruthless savages that had surrounded the sanctified city's natives and kept them oppressed with perpetual swordfights and arson.
>
> Nevertheless, the peace of this nation relies on the private friendships formed in town and country. Polarization leads to unrest, and internal dissent causes failure in public.

Ergo cavete, viri, ne sit sententia discors
sensibus in nostris, ne secta exotica tectis
nascatur conflata odiis, quia fissa voluntas   760
confundit variis arcana biformia fibris.
Quod sapimus coniungat amor, quod vivimus uno
conspiret studio. Nil dissociabile firmum est.

Utque homini atque deo medius intervenit Iesus,
qui sociat mortale patri ne carnea distent   765
spiritui aeterno sitque ut deus unus utrumque,
sic quidquid gerimus mentisque et corporis actu
spiritus unimodis texat conpagibus unus.

Pax plenum virtutis opus, pax summa laborum,
pax belli exacti pretium est pretiumque pericli,   770
sidera pace vigent, consistunt terrea pace.
Nil placitum sine pace deo. Non munus ad aram
cum cupias offerre probat, si turbida fratrem
mens inpacati sub pectoris oderit antro;

nec, si flammicomis Christi pro nomine martyr   775
ignibus insilias servans inamabile votum

So, brave men, be on guard! Let's let no divisive opinion enter our senses, and thus give rise to anomalous factions fueled by secret rifts.

You see, internal divisions muddle competing desires we feel. They challenge convictions.

Let's let our understanding be wedded by love! Let our lives now breathe as one in their aims— because everything atomized crumbles. Hence,

– Just as Jesus effects a transition from God to the human, linking mortality thus to the Father, to see that the Spirit won't be away from the flesh, and so that the two will be *one* God;
– so, let's allow one spirit to interweave all of our efforts—mental and physical actions alike—in a uniform knitwork!

Peace is *the* work of virtue; peace is the sum of our labors. Peace is the prize for the war that you waged and the prize for the peril. Peace enlivens the stars, and peace stabilizes the earthly. Nothing is pleasing to God without peace. He refuses to sanction offerings we'd make at an altar, if our heart's dark recesses don't make peace with a brother, and hate him, our feelings disordered.

Martyr yourself in the name of Christ by leaping upon red tresses of fire!—Even so, if you harbor

bile sub obliqua, pretiosam proderit Iesu
inpendisse animam, meriti quia clausula pax est.
Non inflata tumet, non invidet aemula fratri,
omnia perpetitur patiens atque omnia credit,   780
numquam laesa dolet, cuncta offensacula donat,
occasum lucis venia praecurrere gestit
anxia ne stabilem linquat sol conscius iram.

Quisque litare deo mactatis vult holocaustis,
offerat in primis pacem. Nulla hostia Christo   785
dulcior, hoc solo sancta ad donaria vultum
munere convertens puro oblectatur odore.
Sed tamen et niveis tradit deus ipse columbis
pinnatum tenera plumarum veste colubrum
rimante ingenio docte internoscere mixtum   790

innocuis avibus; latet et lupus ore cruento
lacteolam mentitus ovem sub vellere molli
cruda per agninos exercens funera rictus.
Hac sese occultat Fotinus et Arrius arte
inmanes feritate lupi. Discrimina produnt   795
nostra recensque cruor, quamvis de corpore
    summo,

malevolent wishes out of resentment, then giving a precious soul up for Jesus profits you nothing—because of all merit, *peace* is the end goal.

Peace isn't bloated and swollen, nor does it envy a brother. Peace puts up with everything silently, and it believes all. Never aggrieved or hurt, it pardons every offense; and peace wants forgiveness extended ahead of nightfall, because it fears having sunlight complicit in anger becoming deep-seated.[58]

Anyone wanting to venerate God using holocaust slaughter ought, above all, to offer *peace* instead. No offering to Christ tastes sweeter; for *this* gift alone will He turn His face to a sacred altar and, with pleasure, savor its faultless aroma.

Nevertheless! God *Himself* teaches even the flocks of white doves to skillfully ply some knack for discernment. They notice a serpent flocked with a delicate coating of feathers that's mingling among His innocent birds.

So too the wolf, with his face bathed in blood: he hides underneath the soft, fleece hide of an ivory sheep, yet . . . practices outright murder, disguised by a little lamb's rictus.

These are the wiles that Photínus and Arius use to conceal themselves. Both are merciless, ravening wolves. The defiance and bloodshed we've just incurred—although the injuries *are* superficial—show what a stealthy cabal can accomplish."[59]

quid possit furtiva manus." Gemitum dedit omnis
virtutum populus casu concussus acerbo.

Tum generosa Fides haec subdidit: "Immo,
    secundis
in rebus cesset gemitus. Concordia laesa est,   800
sed defensa Fides; quin et Concordia sospes
germanam comitata Fidem sua vulnera ridet.
Haec mea sola salus, nihil hac mihi triste recepta.
Unum opus egregio restat post bella labori,
o proceres, regni quod tandem pacifer heres   805
belligeri armatae successor inermus et aulae
instituit Solomon, quoniam genitoris anheli
fumarat calido regum de sanguine dextra.

Sanguine nam terso templum fundatur et ara
ponitur, auratis Christi domus ardua tectis.   810
Tunc Hierusales templo inlustrata quietum
suscepit iam diva deum, circumvaga postquam
sedit marmoreis fundata altaribus arca.
¡Surgat et in nostris templum venerabile castris,
omnipotens cuius sanctorum sancta revisat!   815

All the assembled Virtues let out a groan. They're stunned by this bitter reversal.

Then noble Faith speaks up:

"Now, now, in an hour of triumph, groaning must have no place. It is true that Unity's injured, yes, but *Faith* was defended!

Moreover, Unity *lives on yet!* Here beside me—her sister, Faith—she laughs at her wounds. And *that* is my one salvation: we *saved* her, so nothing upsets me.

One final postwar task now awaits your exemplary efforts, captains, a practice that Solomon started. He'd been, at long last, the peaceful heir to a militaristic throne, and disarmed the palace at war he took over. He did so because of his breathless father's hand, which had always reeked of the warm blood of kings.

See, after the blood had been cleared, he erected a temple and built an altar—a towering house of Christ, with gold for its cladding. Soon Jerusalem, glorified by the temple, took in her God in repose. She'd become divine, too, once the nomadic Ark of the Covenant settled down on her platform of marble.

Let's have a sacred temple arise here in *our* camp as well!—a temple whose Holy of Holies omnipotent God can arrive in. Otherwise, what was the

Nam ¿quid terrigenas ferro pepulisse falangas
culparum prodest, hominis si filius arce
aetheris inlapsus purgati corporis urbem
intret inornatam templi splendentis egenus?

Hactenus alternis sudatum est comminus armis; 820
¡munia nunc agitet tacitae toga candida pacis
atque sacris sedem properet discincta iuventus!"

Haec ubi dicta dedit, gradibus regina superbis
desiluit tantique operis Concordia consors
metatura novum iacto fundamine templum.   825
Aurea planitiem spatiis percurrit harundo
dimensis, quadrent ut quattuor undique frontes,
ne commissuris distantibus angulus inpar
argutam mutilet per dissona semetra normam.

Aurorae de parte tribus plaga lucida portis   830
inlustrata patet, triplex aperitur ad austrum
portarum numerus, tris occidualibus offert
ianua trina fores, totiens aquilonis ad axem
panditur alta domus. Nullum illic structile saxum,

use in expelling the phalanx of earthborn Sins with
the point of a sword, if the Son of Man is to come
down out of His heavenly citadel, only to enter the
pristine body's austere city? He *needs* a magnificent
temple!

All this time, it's been hand-to-hand combat
and varying weapons. Now, let the whitened toga
of quieter *peace!* do its duty. Let's get our young
decommissioned and hasten a home for His
presence."

The Construction of a Temple of Peace

Once she has spoken these words, the queen de-
scends by the grandstand steps. In unison, Unity
goes as her partner upon this work, to measure the
site and to lay the new temple foundations.

Over the ground her rod of gold is briskly
surveying measurements, making the four sides
square in their every dimension, lest any incorrect
angles compromise perfect precision: corner-joint
gaps would undoubtedly leave things uneven and
crooked. . . . [60]

Nearest the rising sun, three portals awash in the
light grant access through a resplendent façade. To
the south, there are triple portals opening up; to
the west, three gateways provide a threefold entry,
while on the northern stretch, the cathedral opens
coequally wide. No masonry blocks are in use here;

sed cava per solidum multoque forata dolatu   835
gemma relucenti limen conplectitur arcu
vestibulumque lapis penetrabile concipit unus.

Portarum summis inscripta in postibus auro
nomina apostolici fulgent bis sena senatus.
Spiritus his titulis arcana recondita mentis   840
ambit et electos vocat in praecordia sensus;
quaque hominis natura viget, quam corpore toto
quadrua vis animat, trinis ingressibus aram
cordis adit castisque colit sacraria votis.
Seu pueros sol primus agat, seu fervor ephebos   845
incendat nimius, seu consummabilis aevi
perficiat lux plena viros, sive algida borrae
aetas decrepitam vocet ad pia sacra senectam,
occurrit trinum quadrina ad conpeta nomen,
quod bene discipulis disponit rex duodenis.   850

Quin etiam totidem gemmarum insignia textis
parietibus distincta micant animasque colorum
viventes liquido lux evomit alta profundo.
Ingens chrysolitus nativo interlitus auro
hinc sibi sappirum sociaverat inde beryllum,   855
distantesque nitor medius variabat honores.

rather, each gate is a massive gem that's been hollowed and hewn and bored through. Each encloses a threshold under a sparkling arch, and a single stone comprises each anteroom pass-through.

Gleaming in gold at the top of the portal pillars, apostles' names are inscribed. There's a dozen, which makes for a "senate," and through these labeled inscriptions, the Holy Spirit envelops the mind's dark thoughts—our secrets—and brings on preferable feelings within us. And, where human identity—which is derived from quadruple forces all through the body—thrives, it approaches its inner altar via three doors, and so properly honors the sanctum. Whether it be in the dawn of infancy; or the excessive ardor of teenage years; or the full sunshine of adulthood bringing men into themselves; or the stage when the northerly winds blow cold and recall a decrepit old age to liturgical service: three names occur as one at each end of the four-way piazza—names our King has correctly arranged for His dozen disciples.

Oh, there are also a dozen symbolic and sparkling gemstones separately set in the woven walls. Deep light from their centers throws up their colors' shimmering souls out in every direction.[61] One sensational chrysolite streaked with natural gold is paired with a lapis lazuli here, over there with a beryl, such that the central glimmer keeps changing

Hic calchedon hebes perfunditur ex yacinthi
lumine vicino; nam forte cyanea propter
stagna lapis cohibens ostro fulgebat aquoso.
Sardonicem pingunt ametystina; pingit iaspis   860
sardium iuxta adpositum pulcherque topazon.
Has inter species smaragdina gramine verno
prata virent volvitque vagos lux herbida fluctus.
Te quoque conspicuum structura interserit,
     ardens
chrysoprase, et sidus saxis stellantibus addit.   865

Stridebat gravidis funalis machina vinclis
inmensas rapiens alta ad fastigia gemmas.
At domus interior septem subnixa columnis
crystalli algentis vitrea de rupe recisis
construitur, quarum tegit edita calculus albens   870
in conum caesus capita et sinuamine subter
subductus conchae in speciem, quod mille talentis
margaritum ingens opibusque et censibus hastae
addictis animosa Fides mercata pararat.

Hoc residet solio pollens Sapientia et omne   875
consilium regni celsa disponit ab aula
tutandique hominis leges sub corde retractat.

the glories beside it. Here, there's a dull chalcédony swimming in light from a sapphire neighbor, because (as chance would have it) the neighboring stone holds cyan reservoirs deep inside to flash oystery purple. Amethysts tinge a sardonyx, while a carnelian next to jasper is tinged in turn—with some help from a beautiful topaz. Scattered among these sights are emerald meadows of spring-green grass; their verdant light is rippling wave upon wave out. You've been awarded a prominent presence inside of the structure, fiery chrýsoprase, too. You're included—a star among star-stones.

Outside, the laboring chains of the rope machine creak from the weight of countless enormous gems that they're hustling high to the gable . . .

. . . while the cathedral interior is built so it's resting on seven pillars of frozen, crystalline stone excavated from glassy rock. And, superimposed on their lofty capitals rests a white stone baldachin, cut as a cone which then gradually tapers into a conch-shell look lower down—and this "stone" is an enormous pearl that courageous Faith had acquired at the cost of a thousand talents of silver, once she had auctioned off her possessions.

Here, enshrined on a throne, sits powerful Wisdom, arranging every concern for her kingdom up in her exalted position; and, in her heart, she's considering laws that will insulate man.

In manibus dominae sceptrum non arte politum
sed ligno vivum viridi est, quod stirpe reciso
quamvis nullus alat terreni caespitis umor   880
fronde tamen viret incolumi, tum sanguine tinctis
intertexta rosis candentia lilia miscet
nescia marcenti florem submittere collo.

Huius forma fuit sceptri gestamen Aäron
floriferum, sicco quod germina cortice trudens   885
explicuit tenerum spe pubescente decorem
inque novos subito tumuit virga arida fetus.

Reddimus aeternas, indulgentissime doctor,
grates, Christe, tibi meritosque sacramus honores
ore pio; nam cor vitiorum stercore sordet.   890
Tu nos corporei latebrosa pericula operti
luctantisque animae voluisti agnoscere casus.
Novimus ancipites nebuloso in pectore sensus
sudare alternis conflictibus et variato
pugnarum eventu nunc indole crescere dextra,   895

A scepter is in this sovereign's hands, and it's not finely crafted. Rather, it's living and green, made of wood which, though there's no rootball soil moisture nourishing it (that connection's been severed), nevertheless has bright green leaves all intact; and it features blood-red roses woven together with luminous lilies. Flowers like these are unable to droop, for the stem never withers!

For this scepter, the biblical type is the flowering rod of Aaron, a staff whose dry bark forced out buds and unfolded delicate hopes over time, till they ripened to beautiful blossoms, and, without warning, a dried-up twig was just bursting with new life.

Epilogue: Prudentius Offers This Poem to God in Thanksgiving

O indulgent teacher of ours! We repay You eternal thanks, o Christ, and we offer in tribute this well-deserved honor, spoken through pious lips (for the heart is indecent and fouled with vice). It was You who intended for us to identify hidden perils deep in the flesh and reversals our struggling souls must face.

We have learned that ambiguous feelings clash in our murky breast, in consecutive bouts of conflict; and, as those matchups' outcomes vary, our feelings will either improve and develop, or — when

nunc inclinatis cervicibus [*virtutibus* "Virtues" most
    editions] ad iuga vitae
deteriora trahi seseque addicere noxis
turpibus et propriae iacturam ferre salutis.
O ¡quotiens animam vitiorum peste repulsa
sensimus incaluisse deo, ¡quotiens tepefactum   900
caeleste ingenium post gaudia candida taetro
cessisse stomacho! Fervent bella horrida, fervent
ossibus inclusa. Fremit et discordibus armis
non simplex natura hominis; nam viscera limo
effigiata premunt animum, contra ille sereno   905
editus adflatu nigrantis carcere cordis
aestuat et sordes arta inter vincla recusat.

Spiritibus pugnant variis lux atque tenebrae
distantesque animat duplex substantia vires,
donec praesidio Christus deus adsit et omnes   910
virtutum gemmas conponat sede piata
atque, ubi peccatum regnaverat, aurea templi
atria constituens texat spectamine morum
ornamenta animae, quibus oblectata decoro
aeternum solio dives Sapientia regnet.   915

— FINIS —

our necks bow down in defeat—they are dragged underneath life's yoke for the worse: they addict themselves to destructive perversions, shamefully, and then end up abandoning hope of salvation.

How many times have we felt our soul grown flush with—and for—God, after repulsing the Vices' onslaught! How many times has that beatific commitment faded after the bliss and yielded to loathsome bile! Hideous warfare is raging—raging, and locked in our bones! Human nature is dualistic, it roars with armies at war with each other.

You see, our loins—which are formed from mire—beleaguer our spirit; and, by contrast, the lofty spirit—produced by divine inspiration—rails at our bleak heart's dungeon; even bound tightly in chains, it refuses pollution.

Shifting winds of darkness and light remain locked in a struggle—our dualistic nature animates contrary forces—and they will, until Christ, our God, is here to protect us. Then He will seat all the Virtue-gems in a purified setting. And, in the place where depravity reigned, He'll establish His golden temple enclosures and weave—upon seeing its better behavior—ornaments for the soul, so that affluent Wisdom will relish them as she reigns on her glorious throne, to the end of the ages.

—THE END—

APPENDIX: PLUTARCH'S RECOMMENDATIONS IN OVERVIEW

Baby-Steps Tactics for Resisting Pressure
(paragraphs 5–6 and 8)

1. If someone toasts you and you don't want to drink, just put the glass down.
2. If someone calls you chicken, agree.
3. Trapped in conversation? Just break away.
4. Withhold applause.
5. Practice saying no to irrelevant people (i.e., random strangers you'll never see again).
6. From here, work your way up to refusing requests for money.
7. The general rule: Always choose the better option even when the difference is negligible.

Ten Useful Reflections on Caving
(paragraphs 9–19)

1. Caving exacerbates problems rather than solving them.
2. Silence is an effective answer to an improper request.

3. Quote sayings and quips to soften your refusal.
4. Employ irony as needed when offering a recommendation.
5. Regret is instantaneous, so swallow your (false) pride.
6. Laugh off an underling. That is, use humor—gentle or harsh, as the situation requires—to decline an inappropriate request from below.
7. Guilt-trip an inappropriate request from above. That is, appeal to the petitioner's honor to decline the request. (The line "Please don't ask me that" works well, but even better are the words "I'm surprised you feel comfortable asking me that." That line strikes fear in even the bravest hearts and works like magic.)
8. Addicts show us what *true* resistance to pressure looks like.
9. Welcome criticism from bullies—because criticism is inevitable anyway.
10. Memory (emotional memory, like muscle memory) is the best antidote to caving again.

APPENDIX

The Dire Consequences of Caving
(paragraphs 7–8)

1. money (lending it stupidly)
2. health (choosing a doctor)
3. your children's education (choosing a school)
4. lawsuits (choosing a lawyer not based on merit)
5. your personal beliefs (choosing your religion, your identity, etc.)

ABOUT THIS EDITION

A Note on the Translations

Like the Greek original, the translation of Plutarch is straightforward chatty prose, but it calls for one caveat. Like his hero Plato, Plutarch traffics heavily in the idiom of mental health in a way that is bound to cause confusion today. He frequently calls unpleasant emotions (including dysopia) "diseases" and "illnesses" and "pathologies." But to translate those words literally would sometimes give the wrong impression. For Plutarch, such feelings are not signs of chemical or humoral imbalances or brain disease; they are merely metaphors, as when we speak of "a healthy attitude" or a "mind virus." I have accordingly tweaked his language where it seemed destined to be misleading.[62]

Prudentius's text, by contrast, is a poem. The 68-line preface is in iambic trimeter, which is a meter typically used for fables and the like in Latin. I have translated it as blank verse, which is the corresponding meter in English. The main poem, however, is in "dactylic hexameter." This is the traditional meter used for epic poetry in Greek and

Latin. In it, each line has six beats. These beats emerge from the alternation of long and short syllables in various combinations and patterns. Each line begins on an "up" beat, varies in the center, and then ends the same way, with a stress pattern equivalent to *stráwberry íce cream*. The rhythm is most easily illustrated in English by *Evangeline*, Longfellow's 1847 epyllion on the Expulsion of the Acadians (canto 1):

> **Sóme**what a**párt** from the **víl**lage, and **neár**er the
>   **Bá**sin of **Mí**nas,
> **Bén**edict **Bél**lefon**taíne**, the **weál**thiest **fár**mer of
>   **Gránd**-Pré,
> **Dwélt** on his **goód**ly ácres: and **wíth** him, di**réct**ing
>   his **hoúse**hold,
> **Gén**tle Ev**án**geline **lív**ed, his **chíld**, and the **príde** of
>   the **víl**lage.

Hope's speech in verses 285 and 289–90 is a nice illustration of these rhythms in *Psychomachia*:

> *Désine gránde loquí, frangít deus ómne*
>   *supérbum . . .*
> *pérvulgáta vigét nostrí senténtia Chrísti*
> *scándere céls(a h)umilés et ad íma redíre feróces.*
> **Énd** your grand**í**loquent **tálk**; God **breáks** down
>   **éve**rything **príde**ful . . .

Éveryone, éverywhere, (ha)s heárd and repeáts our
   messíah's pronóuncement:
(*The*) *húmble ascénd to the héights, the aggréssive
   go báck to the bóttom.*

Note that unlike Longfellow's verse or my translation,
in Latin verse—as these samples show—readers must
often disregard the word's natural accent and instead
stress whatever syllable the verse template requires. The
strange clashes produced or avoided by this requirement
are one of the charms that make Latin poetry so worth
reading in the original.

   As with my translation of Ovid in *How to Get Over a
Breakup*, the translation of Prudentius here could be said
to have "surgeon's cuffs." That is, it's printed as prose, but
it replicates the rhythm of the original poem line for line.
My hope is that readers new to Latin poetry will experience the poem's movement subliminally, while students
of classical meters should have no trouble "unbuttoning"
the formatting and restoring the poetry.

   Psychomachia is action-oriented, with all the high
drama of a boxing match, a Hollywood western, or a light
saber duel—and with plenty of humorous touches here
and there. The verses are gorgeous, fluid, and as artificial
as an Auto-Tuned vocal track today. Much of the tension
emerges from the adroit use of end stopping and enjamb-
ment. In the translation, I've sought to imitate those

effects by italicizing a surprising or key word and adding an exclamation point, or with various other punctuation.

A Note on the Texts

The Greek text is that of De Lacy and Einarson 1959, though I've changed paragraphing, preferred variant readings in sections 2, 3, 17, and 18, and silently corrected typos in sections 7, 10, and 13. The Latin text is that of Pelttari 2019, though I've changed some punctuation and ventured to disagree in lines 9 of the preface, 177, 268, 727–28, and 896. For interpretation, I am indebted to the erudite commentaries of Pelttari 2019, Frisch 2020, and Volpe Cacciatore 1994. As in my earlier books in this series, I have freely changed formatting, capitalization, and, for the Latin, I have borrowed punctuation from Spanish to disambiguate questions and exclamations. All subheadings in both translations are my own.

NOTES

Introduction

1 Schaler 2000. As he points out, until recently the word *addiction* always meant "devotion." In classical Latin *addictus* (an addict) meant "slave for money," but by the Renaissance, such as we see in Erasmus's *Praise of Folly*, the metaphorical meaning "devoted to" is clearly in evidence.

2 Golden 2006, xxxiii–iv. The famous post-Renaissance panic in Salem, Massachusetts, in 1692–93 was, therefore, but a drop in the bucket—and a late one at that.

3 Szasz 2010, Szasz 1997, and Conrad and Schneider 1992.

4 Ballard 2021.

5 On Plato's idiosyncratic belief in literal (and therefore blameless) mental illness, see Kenny 1973.

6 *Tusculan Disputations* 3.XI.25.

7 Tsouna 2001.

8 Seneca Epistle 83.10–11 and 83.18; Conrad and Schneider 1992, 76.

9 The anecdote is quoted in this form in Heller 1967, 64.

10 Readers can explore the best illustrations at https://www.e-codices.unifr.ch/en/thumbs/bbb/0264/ (Bern), https://digitalcollections.universiteitleiden.nl /view/item/1935754#page/126/mode/1up (Leiden), https://manuscrits-france-angleterre.org/view3if/pl/ark:/81055 /vdc_100056022455.0x000001/f15 (Cotton), and https:// parker.stanford.edu/parker/catalog/nz663nv2057 (Cambridge). Stramaglia 2007 discusses and illustrates other sorts of proto-comic books from ancient Greece and Rome.

11 La Boétie and Kurz 1997, 37.

12 Bardyn 2018 demonstrates the clear influence of a 1518 dialogue titled *The Court-Hater* (*Misaulus*) by the German Renaissance poet Ulrich von Hutten (1488–1523).

13 Szasz 1991, 1–2. Schopenhauer's remark comes from *The World as Will and Representation*.

Resisting Pressure. Plutarch: *Dysopia (On Caving)*

14 The wit was punning on two meanings of *kore*: (1) "pupil of the eye" and (2) "virgin, maiden." According to Longinus (*On Sublimity* 4), the wit in question was Timaeus of Tauromenium.

15 Plutarch, who took an unusual interest in Egyptian lore, is giving a legendary origin story for the "uraeus," the cobra headdress traditionally worn by Egyptian sovereigns. Bakenranef ruled in the 720s BCE; according to Plutarch's

contemporary Tacitus, he was the pharaoh who expelled the Jews from Egypt (*Histories* 5.3). If Plutarch's text is correct, then the cobra is there to terrorize Bakenranef himself, like the Sword of Damocles. If, however, "harsh" (*chalepo*) is a scribe's mistake for "gentle" (*galeno*), then the cobra is there to terrorize Bakenranef's subjects.

16 Pederastic rape in Greece was (by today's standards) statutory rather than violent, but for an ancient perspective that dispels the fantasy of "consent," see Lucian's dialogue *Ganymede*. And although in English Plutarch may seem vague, his words *malakon* (soft), *pathesi* (experiences), and *paidikes* (boyhood) hint all too clearly at the children in such relationships, who were variously called *malakoi*, *pathikoi*, or *paidika*. The day-to-day social experiences of respectable women in ancient Greece are dramatized in the Roman comedies of Plautus and Terence, while Llewellyn-Jones 2003 documents their use of veils.

17 As Donald Trump notoriously put it, "When you're a star, they let you do it. You can do anything." His one word "let"—which, despite everything else, implies consent—echoes Plutarch's statement here.

18 Here and elsewhere, "dollar" is used for *drachma* and *talent of silver*, the latter being 6,000 drachmas. A single drachma was worth about $50.00; I have rounded amounts off inexactly to convey their metaphorical meaning.

19 Literally, "as far as the altar." We swear by the Bible; Greeks touched an altar.

20 The translation strains to capture the spirit of the bitter punchline. In Greek, Antigonus puns on the man's name, Bias. Instead of saying *Bíanti* (to Bias), Antigonus says *biai . . . kai ananke*, which can mean either (1) "give him the money perforce (*bía*) and of necessity" or (2) "dedicate a talent to Force and Necessity." Corinth had a temple jointly dedicated to Bias and Ananke (Pausanias 2.4.6), so perhaps that is the reference. Since no relevant person named Bias is attested for this period, some editors change the name Bias to Bion and refer it to Bion of Borysthenes, a Cynic philosopher and satirist of the Hellenistic age.

21 A generation or two before Plutarch, Seneca had reported this same anecdote in *How to Give* (p. 69 = *On Benefits* 2.16.2). Seneca characterizes Antigonus's responses as "sophistry," but ultimately endorses them. Cynics were monks avant la lettre; they cultivated a life of poverty. Hence if a Cynic hates money as he claims, reasons Seneca, then it's insupportable for him to also ask for it. In *How to Tell a Joke*, Quintilian, Plutarch's ten-year-younger contemporary, also recommends the use of humor to deflect an improper request. He cites two similar quips allegedly made by the emperor Augustus (pp. 227 and 247).

22 Seneca takes a similar view of anger in *How to Keep Your Cool*: "There is no emotion more eager for vengeance than anger, and for that very reason, none *less* suited to the taking of vengeance" (p. 23 = *De Ira* 1.12.5).

23 They're exposed as having no money because they end up having to borrow money themselves.

24 As noted in the introduction, this throwaway joke may be the first link in a chain that ends with Mahatma Gandhi, Martin Luther King Jr., and the principle of nonviolent resistance. (Indeed, a widely quoted remark of Gandhi's comes very close: "There is in the English language a very potent word—all languages have it: 'No.'")

25 In both quotations, Plutarch is riffing on verses from tragedy (the first unknown, the second from Euripides's *Pirithous*). Quintilian recommends and illustrates this procedure in *How to Tell a Joke* (pp. 249–53). In the first, Plutarch reinterprets *argyros* (silver) as *argyrion* (cash, like French *argent*) and *xenos* (meaning "stranger") as "friend."

26 This sentence shows that Plutarch thinks of dysopia (or at least the verb) as the action of caving as well as the unpleasant emotion that precipitates it.

27 Theocritus of Chios was a famous wit of the fourth century. The same joke appears in the late Greek-Roman joke book known as *Philogelos*, #150 (p. 83 Thierfelder). In the translation of Bill Berg (in *Philogelos: The Laugh Addict* [2008, self-published]),

A quick study is in the public bath. Two guys ask to borrow one of his strigils for scraping the olive oil off their bodies. One of them is a stranger, the other he recognizes as a thief. To the one he says, 'No deal; I don't know you.' To the other: 'No deal; I know you.'

28 Plutarch is referring to the fastidious avoidance of "hiatus," wherein a vowel fails to contract with the following vowel. Pedants in Plutarch's time sought to avoid hiatus at all costs. English has no such phenomenon, but an analogue may be the horror some feel at split infinitives, sentences that end with a preposition, or using contractions in academic writing.

29 In order to amplify his indignation, Plutarch is making a pun on *phaulos* and *philos* that is hard to capture in translation. As in the English words *oenophile* (a connoisseur of wine), *bibliophile* (books), and *turophile* (cheese), many Greek words for penchants contain the root *phil-* (meaning *love*). Occasionally, as here, these compounds suggest an "unhealthy" obsession, as in *pedophile* (children—as in note 16 above), *necrophile* (corpses), and *coprophile* (don't ask). Plutarch's three examples here are *philargyros* (cash-loving, i.e., greedy), *philotimos* (honor-loving, i.e., status-seeking), and *philarchos* (command-loving, i.e., power-hungry). All such *philos* people are "addicts." Plutarch's word for such people is *phaulos*, a word that basically means "perverse" or "crummy" (as with the hotel in section 8). As *philos* means "addicted," he implies, so *phaulos* means "addled."

30 I follow Pohlenz's text here.

31 Obsopoeus has a memorable description of such a person in *How to Drink* (p. 229). Plutarch's climactic sentence here calls back to the etymology of *dysopia* (face, countenance) in section 1.

32 Bion's riddle entails two puns in Greek: (1) *ous* (ear; handle of an amphora) and (2) *metapherein* (transfer; change).

33 Antisthenes wrote a lost book of moral instruction titled *Hercules*.

34 An impressive ambiguity: (1) it is by my poetry (efforts, action) that you are telling the truth, and (2) I will do my best to ensure you're telling the truth.

Slaying Your Demons

35 Prudentius turns the mysterious Melchizedek of Genesis 14:18–20 into the archetypal "Man with No Name."

36 The mystic sum stands for Jesus. In Greek, the number 318 is written TIH, of which the first digit resembles a cross, while the second and third are the same as the first two letters of Jesus's name in Greek, ΙΗΣΟΥΣ.

37 Prudentius's conception of the mind is strikingly similar to the model Sigmund Freud would envision fifteen centuries later, and the strategy he recommends for besting vice is the very one whereby Freud overthrew the repressive morality of the nineteenth century. As Stefan

Zweig (1881–1942), who was an eyewitness to Freud's triumph, describes it:

> Free from illusions, without faith in progress, relentless, and radical, Freud showed that the impulsive energy of the libido, though condemned by the moralists, was an indestructible part of the human organism, a force that could not be annulled so long as life and breath remained, and that *the best way of dealing with it was to lift it into the conscious* where its activities would be free from danger. The old method had aimed at covering it up. He aimed at its revealment. Where others had cloaked it, he wanted to lay it bare; where others had ignored it, he wanted to identify it. *No one can bridle impulses without perceiving them clearly; no one can master demons unless he summons them forth from their lurking-places and looks them boldly in the face.* (261–62, emphasis added)

38 As in much of the ancient Mediterranean, traditional Roman religion before Christianity was based on animal sacrifice.

39 The "original bloodline" in this crabbed sentence refers to Adam.

40 These awkward sentences in brackets seem to be interpolated.

41 A remarkable reading of the Expulsion from Eden. In Pride's view, Adam has been (as we say today)

"redpilled." Her perspective comes very close to that of Thomas Szasz (2003, 175–81): "The parable of the Fall illustrates this fight to the death between control and self-control. Did Eve, tempted by the Serpent, seduce Adam, who then lost control of himself and succumbed to evil? Or did Adam, facing a choice between obedience to the authority of God and his own destiny, choose self-control?" (Readers interested in Szasz's perspective on willpower, virtue, and vice are advised to read the previous chapter in Szasz 2003, "Temptation and Temperance.")

42 Matthew 23:12: "For those who exalt themselves will be humbled, and those who humble themselves will be exalted."

43 The phrase "willing slaves" (*servire volens*) evokes the title of La Boétie's essay *On Voluntary Servitude*. (See the introduction.)

44 Falernian was the most famous wine of antiquity, and a cantharus was a trophy cup used in rowdy drinking (for details, see my *How to Drink*).

45 Manna. The parenthesis ("indeed, flown!") translates Prudentius's pun on *avis* (grandfathers) and *avis* (bird). The latter word alludes to the quails that, according to Exodus 16:13, flew to the Israelites when they wearied of eating manna.

46 With its appeal to nobility, this moving plea evokes the all-too-familiar request a loved one makes of an addict spiraling out of control.

47 These arresting lines are some of the most profound in the poem. Temperance turns a story in 1 Samuel 15 into a double lesson about our struggle against vice. In the biblical account, Samuel killed the captured king of the Amalekites and forbade Saul from taking any of the spoils. In Temperance's account here, the "spoils" first allude to the problem of temptation: when faced with something that looks good but is bad for us (drugs or alcohol, say), should we "touch" or try it, just once? Or should we prohibit the substance entirely, as Samuel did? And second, the surviving "king" is the Astyanax problem, like leaving embers in a fire: should we spare an enemy to fight another day? Or kill him in custody and be done with it? Interestingly, Temperance combines both problems in a pun (*praeda superstes*) that refers to both (1) a "surviving stash" of goods that remains after others have helped themselves to it, which will perpetually tempt (*poscat*) us, and (2) a malicious king "taken alive," and hence a symbol for our neverending struggle against our demons (addictions, vices). Incidentally, the "noble spirits" are (1) the better angels of our nature, i.e., our better inclinations, and (2) the aristocratic line of Judah and kings and Jesus, which should inspire us.

48 The phrase *dulce malum* (sweet evil, i.e., vice, sin) puns on *dulce mālum* (sweet apple), thereby alluding to Eve's fateful choice in the Garden of Eden.

49 In 1 Samuel 14:24–45, Jonathan accidentally disobeys his father's order to abstain from food. The penalty was death, but he confessed his error and was spared.

50 Note that although *temperance* and *temptress* sound alike in English, they do not in Latin, and should not be confused.

51 It would appear that Temperance is not holding the cross upright, like some Hollywood priest attempting an exorcism, but rather butting it perpendicular up against her shoulder and pretending the cross is a crossbow. (What the horses misinterpret as a muzzle is in fact the gilded or jeweled top of the cross.)

52 In Joshua 7, an Israelite soldier named Achan is stoned for disobeying orders and stealing items from the spoils of Jericho. (In the late German Renaissance, a Neolatin poet named Joannes Burmeister adapted Plautus's *Aulularia* to dramatize his story.)

53 Judah's coethnics are Christians (descended from Judah by way of Christ).

54 Her Latin name, Operatio, resembles the Latin name of Reason, Ratio, and suggests an inherent connection between the two. In Christian understanding, "action" is equivalent to "good works."

55 The parting of the Red Sea into two "jaws" appears in Exodus 15:1–21.

56 Prudentius's original readers would have recognized Disunity's heretical views about the nature of God as those preached by some of their early Christian contemporaries—specifically Arius, Marcion, Sabellius, the Manicheans, and either Gnostic or Neoplatonic lore. In the Bible, Belial is the wicked or worthless one, a devil who leads men into dissolution.

57. Editors use daggers (†) to signal that the text of lines 727–28 is hopelessly corrupt. A later reader trying to make sense of them added his own line, 729, which editors have since identified and deleted as an interpolation.

58 Ephesians 4:26: "Do not let the sun go down while you are still angry."

59 Photinus of Ankara (died 376) denied the divinity of Jesus and taught that God was only one person. Before him, Arius (206–336) had taught that the Father was greater than the Son. Both were influential in their times.

60 The rod of gold is an allusion to Revelation 21:15–16. As *Psychomachia* began with stories from Genesis, so it ends with allusions to the Book of Revelation. From here on out, the temple is described as complete.

61 The dozen symbolic gemstones about to be named are traditional, since they're also found on Aaron's breastplate in Exodus 28:17–21 and the foundation walls of the "celestial New Jerusalem" in Revelation 21:10–27. What do they symbolize here? Presumably, Prudentius might say, whatever they symbolize there: the tribes of Israel, the apostles, properties of the divine essence, or all of the above.

About This Edition

62 Again, for Plato's use of mental health metaphors, see Kenney 1973 (as in note 5).

BIBLIOGRAPHY

Ballard, Jamie. 2021. "Two in Five Americans Say Ghosts Exist—and One in Five Say They've Encountered One." YouGov.com. Online at https://tinyurl.com/AmericanDemons.

Bardyn, Christophe. 2018. "La Boétie contre les courtisans." *L'Enseignement philosophique* 68a1:25–39.

Becchi, Francesco. 1996. "Riflessioni sul Περὶ δυσωπίας di Plutarco." *Prometheus* 22:274–80.

Conrad, Peter, and Joseph W. Schneider. 1992. *Deviance and Medicalization: From Badness to Sickness*. 2nd ed. Philadelphia: Temple University Press.

Curtius, Quintus, trans. 2023. *Cicero: On the Nature of the Gods*. Charleston: Fortress of the Mind Publications.

De Lacy, Phillip H., and Benedict Einarson, eds. 1959. *Plutarch: Moralia*, vol. 7. Cambridge, MA: Harvard University Press. (Loeb)

Erasmus, Desiderius, trans. 1526. *Plutarchus Chaeroneus: De vitiosa verecundia*. Basel: apud Joannem Frobenium.

Frisch, Magnus, ed. and trans. 2020. *Prudentius, ›Psychomachia‹. Einleitung, Text, Übersetzung und Kommentar*. Berlin; Boston: De Gruyter.

Golden, Richard M., ed. 2006. *Encyclopedia of Witchcraft: The Western Tradition*, vol. 1. Santa Barbara: ABC-CLIO.

Heller, Erich. 1967. "A Symposium: Assessment of the Man and the Philosopher." In *Ludwig Wittgenstein: The Man and His Philosophy*, edited by K. T. Fann, 64–66. New York: Dell, Delta Books.

Kenny, Anthony. 1973. "Mental Health in Plato's Republic." In *The Anatomy of the Soul: Historical Essays in the Philosophy of Mind*, 1–27. New York: Barnes & Noble.

La Boétie, Étienne de, and Harry Kurz. 1997. *The Politics of Obedience: The Discourse of Voluntary Servitude*. With an introduction by Murray N. Rothbard. 2nd ed. Montreal: Black Rose Books.

Llewellyn-Jones, Lloyd. 2003. *Aphrodite's Tortoise: The Veiled Woman of Ancient Greece*. Swansea: Classical Press of Wales.

Pelttari, Aaron, ed. 2019. *The Psychomachia of Prudentius: Text, Commentary, and Glossary*. Norman: University of Oklahoma Press.

Schaler, Jeffrey. 2000. *Addiction Is a Choice*. Chicago: Open Court.

Stramaglia, Antonio. 2007. "Il fumetto e le sue potenzialità mediatiche nel mondo greco-latino." In *Escuela y literatura en Grecia antigua,* edited by J. A. Fernández Delgado, F. Pordomingo, and A. Stramaglia, 577–643. Frosinone: Edizioni dell'Università degli Studi di Cassino.

Szasz, Thomas. 1991. [1970]. *Ideology and Insanity: Essays on the Psychiatric Dehumanization of Man.* 2nd ed. Syracuse: Syracuse University Press.

Szasz, Thomas. 1997. [1970]. *The Manufacture of Madness: A Comparative Study of the Inquisition and the Mental Health Movement.* 2nd ed. Syracuse: Syracuse University Press.

Szasz, Thomas. 2003. [1974]. *Ceremonial Chemistry: The Ritual Persecution of Drugs, Addicts, and Pushers.* 2nd ed. Syracuse: Syracuse University Press.

Szasz, Thomas. 2010. [1961]. *The Myth of Mental Illness: Foundations of a Theory of Personal Conduct.* 2nd ed. New York: Harper Perennial.

Tsouna, Voula. 2001. "Philodemus on the Therapy of Vice." In *Oxford Studies in Ancient Philosophy,* vol. 21, edited by David Sedley, 234–58. Oxford: Clarendon Press.

Volpe Cacciatore, Paola, ed. 1994. *Plutarco: L'eccessiva arrendevolezza.* Naples: M. d'Auria.

Zweig, Stefan. 1932. *Mental Healers.* Translated by Eden and Cedar Paul. New York: Viking Press.